MONEY—Use It or Lose It

MONEY—USE IT or LOSE IT

FINANCIAL SUCCESS:
A COMMON-SENSE APPROACH

Vern Hayden, CFP

With a Foreword by
Ronald A. Melanson, CFP
President
International Association of Financial Planners
1979–1980

Hayden House Publishing Company
68 Mitchell Boulevard
San Rafael, California 94903

Printed in the United States of America
ISBN 0-937002-00-0
Library of Congress Card No. 80-83414
Book Design by Joe Roter
Typesetting by Franciscan Type

To

My Dad
My Mom

and

My entrepreneurial daughter Kirsten, who at
the age of ten charged me 7 percent interest to
borrow $1 from her piggy bank

and

Erik

Contents

Preface

Too often, from a money standpoint, we just live day to day, week to week, or month to month. For numerous reasons, we do not plan ahead. Many of us, for instance, assume that we will move up the ladder of success and that money will flow in and that "it" will take care of "itself."

Well, "it" won't take care of "itself." If you want a secure financial future, "it" requires *attention* and *management*. You must apply the same amount of effort to make your money grow that you applied in earning it.

The theme of this book is that if you earn an income and if you *regularly* save a small amount of that income and if you apply the ideas and strategies brought forth in this book, you can become financially independent. It will take time and perseverance, but it will happen.

The purpose of this book is to give you an overview of the *process* that will help you to make a profit with *your* money. Regardless of the state of the economy, you should have a financial plan that will enable you to survive and prosper.

The thrust of this book is to *take action* to improve your *financial situation.* The tools are available to everyone. Use them and secure your financial future.

I suggest that you seek assistance in this endeavor from the "new professional," the *financial planner.*

V.C.H.

San Rafael, California
July 4, 1980

Acknowledgments

The writing of this book has benefited from my personal friendships and professional associations with many people. They have contributed directly and indirectly, and they have been so numerous that it is impossible to name them all. But I must mention some; for those I have unintentionally omitted I only hope they can empathize with the treachery of the task of acknowledging a few.

Without belaboring the various reasons I would simply like to express my deep gratitude to the following people.

Bill Conover	George Huff
John Croxall	Bob Kennedy
Alan Douglass	Ron Melanson
Gordon Gaddy	John Shellenberger

— and to the International Association of Financial Planners for their warm, inspiring, and instructive association.

— and a special tribute to Nickie Sherley, whose idea it was to write this book and who made me believe what I was doing for a few could help many. She spent countless hours helping and encouraging me.

The following people also deserve special recognition and thanks for their tremendous work on the creative mechanics and artistry in getting this book published: Andrew Nickerson, Howard Chandler, W. L. Parker, and Lesley Pollack (the cartoons). They deserve credit, but have no responsibility for this book's content.

V.C.H.

Foreword

By Ronald A. Melanson, *Certified Financial Planner;* President,
International Association of Financial Planners

Often we find ourselves looking for a plan that will change our
lives decidedly for the better. Vern Hayden's book *Money—Use It
or Lose It* is such a plan if financial independence is your goal.
Get ready for some reading that will make plenty of common
sense. This is straight talk. He translates for you most of the
complex financial jargon emanating from the specialized sectors
of the investment, insurance, banking, legal, and accounting
communities. His down-to-earth approach takes out the mystery
and puts in the confidence needed to make the right financial
decisions.

What you would like to have is a financial plan—one that works
effectively, that makes you feel comfortable, that is understandable, flexible, and easily managed. Such a financial plan can be a
reality for you. Self-discipline and attention to detail are needed.
The big key is that you must really *want* it. Use this book and you
will be definitely on the right path to having your own financial
plan.

Vern Hayden has a special humanistic approach to his work. He
is a dedicated professional who loves what he does. He is highly
respected by his colleages within this new financial planning
industry. The concept of "total financial planning" began just
about the time Vern Hayden started his career in 1968. He is
considered one of the leading innovators and spokesmen of his
profession.

You can be certain—Vern Hayden values you, his reader, as he values his personal financial-planning clients. He is the kind of person who knows the word "commitment," and is not afraid to become personally involved. Your financial concerns and frustrations are his challenge to solve.

You will find Vern Hayden to be a person who reveals to you with clarity all that he knows and has experienced. He wants you to learn and to be comfortable with your financial decisions. He will not make these decisions for you. His advice provides you with the space to accept fully the responsibility for your own financial affairs. Above all, he wants you to enjoy the Hayden Financial System, which transforms what might have been overly complex financial methods into a system that is simple, workable and truly understandable.

Money—Use It or Lose It gives you concise information and a perfected technique you can apply in your financial life right now. Numerous examples make it all work for you.

You may soon discover that having such a plan, understanding how it works and successfully managing and updating it, will give you a fine sense of personal accomplishment—a good feeling, and well deserved.

I happen to be one of those people who believes that happiness and success do not just happen to someone—they happen when opportunity meets preparation.

May your opportunities be plentiful—and through planning, may you achieve much success and happiness.

July 12, 1980

MONEY—Use It or Lose It

Prologue

Use this book as you would use a nation-wide road map that depicts only main highways. And as you would turn to more detailed maps for the streets in cities, so likewise you need more detailed financial maps that you can obtain through qualified financial planners. No book alone can give you all the financial information you may desire.

Your financial independence will start when you begin to follow the broad design of the strategies discussed in this book.

After you have built up protection for unforeseeable events such as disability, you are ready to begin tax and investment strategies and to pinpoint specific areas with your financial advisers.

There are six things you can do with your money: spend it, bury it, lend it, give it away, gamble it, or invest it. Of the six, only investing it safely and wisely and protecting yourself while doing so will keep you from losing it.

When you accomplish that, then my goal in writing this book will have been achieved.

PART ONE **YOUR MONEY—
THE TIMES—
YOUR LIFE**

Chapter 1 Your Money

Let's talk about money. *Your* money. No one expects you to work for nothing. There may be some disagreement as to how much money you should receive for the work you do, but you can work that out or go to work somewhere else. Having enough (whatever that elusive word means to you) money is not bad! At times, not having enough can be very bad indeed. Sophie Tucker once said, "I've been rich and I've been poor, and believe me, rich is better."

Very few people in our society have sufficient talent and skills to get rich by being paid enough for what they do. Thus, if you want to be wealthy, you need to start letting your money work for you.

Some of your money undoubtedly is working, earning you more money. *Or is it, really? Is it earning all that it could and should earn?* Most of this book is about those questions and the answers to them—and about how to make the answers *yes.*

If you ask the questions about the money in your checking account the answer may be *no.* It is not the custom for banks to pay you for keeping your money in a checking account— checking accounts earn no interest or relatively little. Indeed, some banks charge customers for keeping their money in checking accounts.

If you ask the questions about the money in your passbook savings account, the answer is also likely to be *no.* Passbook savings accounts do pay their owners interest (5½ percent as this is written), but you need to have most of your money earning more than 5½ percent.

If you ask the questions about the money in your life-insurance policies, the answer is almost surely *no*. The money at work in them is earning you interest, but probably at even lower rates than the money in a passbook savings account.

If you have money invested in securities—stocks, bonds, mutual funds, others—these may or may not be earning you money at a higher rate than bank accounts or insurance policies. But still, are they earning you enough? Are they earning what your money could earn? Are they earning what you need? Maybe *yes*, maybe *no*.

If you feel or suspect that the answers are *no*, you may ask what the bankers or the insurance companies or the corporations or the governments that issued the stocks and bonds are doing with your money. Are they paying themselves too much for the services they are performing in keeping your money safe? Are they paying you less than they should? Are they even perhaps, cheating you? Certainly they are earning money for themselves with your money that is in their care—that would be entirely fair. *But how do you come out after they handle your money and pay you dividends or interest, and after you pay the taxes on the return your money earns?*

Before these money-handling institutions can begin to do their work, you have to earn the money, pay taxes on it, and deposit it in their care. Suppose you want to deposit some of your income in a bank and get a certificate of deposit that will pay you 9-percent interest on your money. Suppose you are in the 30-percent bracket for federal income tax (ignore state income taxes for the moment). Suppose you designate $5,000 from your income to buy that certificate. Now, read the arithmetic in the table on page 7.

Do those numbers stun you? You started out to save $5,000 of your income, but out of it you had to hold aside $1,500 to pay income taxes on it so only $3,500 went into the certificate. Then at the end of the year during which your $3,500 investment earned $315 you had to pay $94.50 more taxes on these earnings; that brought the investment's earnings down to $220.50. And while taxes were eating your money's earnings, a 10-percent inflation rate was eating your money itself—that is, the goods or services you could have bought at the start of the year with

How Much Does It Cost To Save Money?

	$5,000.00	Income designated for savings
−	1,500.00	Federal taxes (30-percent tax bracket)
	3,500.00	After-tax dollars—the dollars invested
×	.09	Interest rate (9 percent)
	315.00	Interest earned
−	94.50	Tax on interest
	220.50	Balance of interest (after taxes)
−	(350.00)	10-percent inflation on $3,500
−	129.50	Negative balance after taxes and inflation
	$3,500.00	After-tax dollars—the dollars invested
−	(129.50)	Negative balance after taxes and inflation
	3,370.50	Balance of the original $5,000 designated for savings
	$5,000.00	The original amount you designated for savings
−	3,370.50	Balance left after adding the interest and subtracting the taxes and inflation
	$1,629.50	*Your cost* for wanting to save $5,000

$3,500 would cost you $350 more at the end of the year. That $350 is a loss that has to be subtracted from the $220.50 of net earnings, and hence "earnings after taxes and inflation" is a net loss —a negative quantity of $129.50. When this loss is taken off the $3,500, you arrive at the end of the year with only $3,370.50. Another subtraction reveals that taxes and inflation have cost you $1,629.50 because you undertook to save $5,000 a year earlier.

And those numbers could be even more distressing. The tax bite could be worse—most states take a state income tax and some cities a city income tax that would cut down the after-tax dollars to less than $3,500. The interest earned could be less than 9 percent. The inflation rate could be worse than 10 percent—in 1980 it most decidedly was worse.

However, there are ways—legal and proper ways—to keep some of your money out of the reach of the income-tax people. You *can* get higher than 9-percent interest on your investments. You *can* put your money into investments where the numbers grow so they can keep ahead of inflation. You need a sound financial plan.

Chapter 2 Inflation and the Times

Our money has taken quite a few bruises over the last several years.

Remember when you went to the post office and bought a hundred post cards for a dollar? They were called "penny" post cards. (Sometimes, they still are.) In 1951 the price doubled, to 2¢ each or 50 for a dollar. Today, they cost 10¢ each and, by the time you read this, they may cost even more. Look at what has happened to your buying power in relation to the "penny" post card. That has been a 90-percent drop between 1951 and 1980 in the purchasing price of the dollar used to buy post cards. Do you realize how much you would have had to make each year since 1951 to make up for this 90-percent drop in your buying power? You would have had to get an 8½-percent compounded tax-free return on your money. And in 1951, savings and loan companies were paying only about 3-percent interest.

A milk shake cost about a dime in 1942. Recently, I paid about $1.25 for a shake. That change demands about a 7-percent compounded tax-free return on your money to keep up with inflation, that is, with your loss in buying power.

Thirty years ago, I used to walk down to Brown's barber shop with my dad, and Mr. Brown would cut my hair for 50¢. These days it's a bargain if I find a barber (hair stylist) who'll cut my hair for $10. To equal that increase, you would have needed to invest your 50¢ over the years at 11-percent compounded tax-free interest.

The products themselves have not changed. The "penny" post cards are the same size (though they take longer to get to their destination). The milk shake is neither colder nor larger nor sweeter. And the barber (excuse me, the hair stylist), in my case, is actually cutting less hair.

Although it is enlightening to review these skyrocketing costs, it is also very painful. But these are the financial facts of life. Realizing them may help you to stop just complaining about the situation and to start taking the necessary steps toward changing your financial picture.

HOW INFLATION WORKS

Let's take a look at how inflation steals your money.

If 100 apples cost $100, then each apple costs $1. If you remove 50 apples and keep the price for the remaining 50 at $100, the cost of each apple has inflated to $2.

Now, the banking system generates 300 new dollars and adds these to the money already chasing the 50 apples. We now have $400 in the money supply, but only 50 apples for the $400 to buy. Thus each apple now is priced at $8.

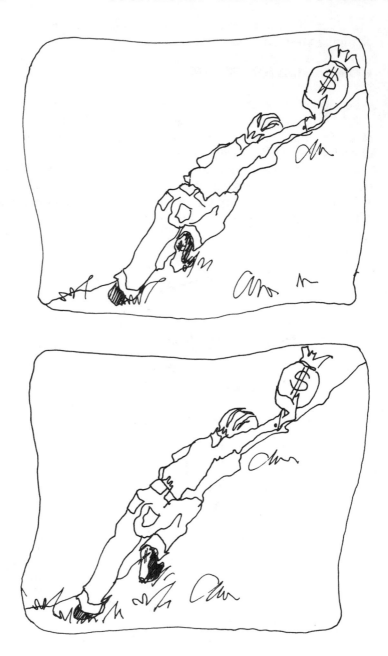

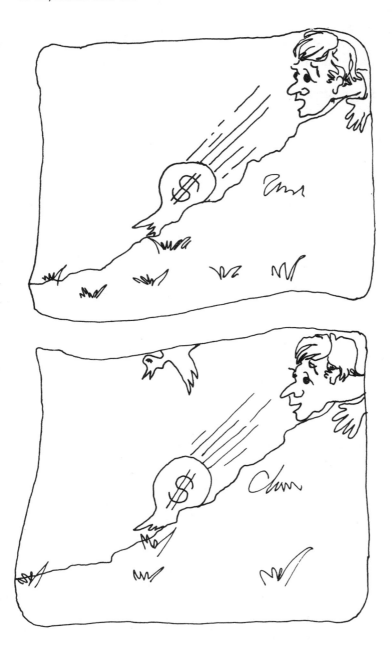

That's how prices rise. The laws of supply and demand are in force. The main reason for the inflated prices is the introduction of *new money* into the market place to purchase *the same amount* of goods.

If post cards and milk shakes and haircuts and apples don't impress you, you may prefer to look at some figures the United States government collects and publishes. These show changes in what is called the Consumer Price Index, the CPI for short. As the CPI goes up, the buying power of the dollar goes down.

Inflation: 1967 to 1978*

| Year | Consumer Price Index | | Purchasing Power of the Dollar |
	Index	Percent Increase	
1967	100.0	—	1.000
1968	104.2	4.2	.960
1969	109.8	5.4	.911
1970	116.3	5.9	.860
1971	121.3	4.3	.824
1972	125.3	3.3	.799
1973	133.1	6.2	.752
1974	147.7	11.0	.677
1975	161.2	9.1	.620
1976	170.5	5.8	.587
1977	181.5	6.5	.551
1978	195.3	9.7	.493

*Figures are from published reports. The changes shown in the CPI and the dollar purchasing power are not in exact agreement.

The Consumer Price Index is often described as the price of a typical basket of goods and services (if you can imagine services in a basket). The market-basket concept is intended to get clear of the confusions arising from various individual items in the basket. The price of meat may rise faster than the price of apartment rents (or the other ways around); the price of gasoline may go up faster than the price of fresh vegetables; and so on. The price of the CPI basket was 100 in 1967; at the end of 1978 it was about 195.

You can look at the numbers which indicate the inflation in the twelve-year table of Consumer Price Indices for the years 1967 through 1978. Two columns in the table show the changes in the

CPI; one column shows the changes (declines) in the value of the dollar, that is, in its purchasing power. The table doesn't show the story after 1978. But if you want some interim facts, the CPI rose more than 12 points in 1979 and seems on the way toward rising more than 12 points in 1980.

What the table does show is that you will lose if you try to just keep your money; it goes down in value. Plainly, you need to invest your money in a way that will build up numbers big enough to overcome that downward inflationary slide. You also need (this was the point developed in Chapter 1) to build the numbers big enough to heal your money after the tax bite has been taken out of it. We can measure the tax bite and the inflation bite. Now we can go on to examine the need—what you need to do if your money is to grow in numbers and hold or gain in value.

In Greek mythology, Sisyphus was given the fate of pushing a boulder up hill. When he paused to take a breath the rock would roll back down to the bottom. Sisyphus would then have to start his eternal push all over again. Many people feel that in their finances they have much in common with Sisyphus. In this book I am going to show you how to push that rock all the way to the top of the mountain and keep it there.

Chapter 3 **The Life Cycle**

Life is a rainbow. We start with zero. We proceed onward through our young and then through our creative years. If we plan and do enough of the right things financially along the way, we can end up with the pot of gold. The planning and the doing are what can color life financially as bright as any rainbow. But they require some work on your part.

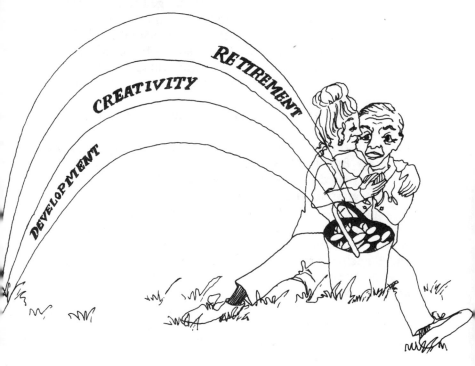

You spend 12 to 18 or more years of your life going to school learning how to *acquire* money. But nowhere in our educational system are you taught how to *use* it effectively. How many 18-year-olds know what a certificate of deposit is? Pitifully few.

Some time after age 18 you make one of the biggest investments of your life—you buy a house. You do it with hardly any knowledge of investments or tax benefits. And if you need help or advice, whom do you ask? Usually the agent who is selling you the property—the one who has the most to gain from your lack of expertise. If that agent is not honest, asking his help is much like asking the fox to guard the hen house. People often make far too many of their money decisions wearing a financial blindfold because they lack knowledge.

People come to me as they near retirement and ask me to "make everything right." I can remove their blindfolds, but often they have been too long in the dark. They seem sunstruck by the answers I give them about how to improve their financial lives. "Why didn't someone tell me this before?" is the question I usually hear. It is never too late to change the strategy of your money-game decisions. But obviously, the sooner you make these changes the better. Other than discipline, the single greatest hazard in implementing a sound financial strategy is *procrastination.* To clear the hurdle of procrastination requires that you start now, make the right decisions, and then take definite action to support them.

If your age is anywhere between 22 and 65, you can create good retirement years. As an example, consider my female client in her early thirties who was earning about $700 a month as a secretary. By careful use of her money during the last four years, she has created a net worth of about $140,000. She is well on her way toward building up a fine block of capital.

Granted, the secretary had some small income beyond her salary, she had loan guarantees, she invested a great amount of work—"sweat equity." And she had exceptional good luck. But she did achieve the gain, and she did so by sound methods that any person could use—including an executive whom she outdid and who will be mentioned next.

Consider, then, the executive who recently came to me for financial help. He was earning $100,000 a year and had been doing so for several years. You figure he had to be rich, right? Wrong! the secretary was the wealthier.

The executive loved the flashy life. He loved fast cars and—among other things—not fast enough horses. Because he had spent his money on fun and taxes had taken the rest, his total assets were an unbelievably low $15,000.

To increase his assets I performed financial surgery on his way of life (easy for me but difficult for him) and he is now making good progress toward building his net worth. And to keep up his spirits as he lives a more Spartan and austere life, I tell him that if he keeps up the good work for a few years he will *almost* be able to live in the style that he was growing accustomed to.

According to the Department of Health and Human Services, out of every 10 men who are 65 or older:

> 13 work full time
> 23 work part time
> 64 are retired

Of the 64 who are retired, *61 have incomes of less than $5,000 a year!* That is poverty.

Don't be one of those people who receive a gold watch at retirement and then later don't have enough money to have it repaired. Start making financial plans now! Start thinking now about financial planning. Later in this book, I'll tell you how to select a financial planner.

Theme:

> People don't plan to fail
> . . . they fail to plan

Chapter 4 **The Three Financial Building Blocks**

To build a solid financial planning program, you need these three building blocks:

1. Short-and long-range goals
2. A financial statement
3. A cash-flow analysis

THE IMPORTANCE OF GOALS

One of the many facts that I have learned from my seminars is that, among the people attending, only about two in a hundred have *written goals*, while almost all have *written wills*. That means approximately 98 percent have a plan for *dying*, but only 2 percent have a plan for *living*.

Following is a sample list of goals. Read them over and then plan to fill in your own goals on the nearby pages. Talk these goals over with the people closest to you. If you are married, you will be surprised at what you learn from and about your spouse's goals.

You may find that some of the goals and objectives you thought you shared are not the same at all. And as you list and discuss your goals, remember that there is no such thing as a "dumb" goal.

Your goals will work if:

1. They are attainable.
2. Progress toward them can be measured.
3. They are challenging.

A SAMPLE LIST OF GOALS

Short-Range Goals

- To take a two-week vacation in August
- To organize my cash flow and balance it once a month
- To spend more time with my family
- To take a class in backpacking
- To play racquetball twice a week
- To lose three pounds a month for five months
- To have an annual physical checkup
- To save $200 a month
- To sell the car and buy a more economical one by September
- To refinish the chair
- To find a good financial planner by April

Long-Range Goals

- To change jobs within two years
- To buy a new house within three years
- To send the children to college
- To find a way to reduce my income taxes each year
- To take a trip around the United States in two years
- To have $2,000 income per month at age 65—in the equivalent of today's dollars
- To start my own business in five years

Your List of Short-Range Goals

_____

_____

_____

_____

_____

_____

_____

_____

_____

_____

_____

_____

_____

_____

Your List of Long-Range Goals

_____

_____

_____

_____

_____

_____

_____

_____

_____

_____

_____

_____

_____

_____

_____

_____

_____

_____

_____

_____

ACHIEVING YOUR GOALS

Once you have put your goals into writing, you need to plan how you are going to reach each one. Write each goal, alone, at the top of a blank page. On every goal page, write how you will go about reaching that goal—and when. Be very specific about the target date for reaching the goal. Have your calendar or date book handy so you can put the goal on the date space or the date page.

Now you have a better idea of what you want in life (maybe for the very first time). Before now, you just thought you knew. Now that you've written the goals down, *you know you do.*

Review your short-range goals once a week and your long-range goals at least once a month. Start measuring your progress. Refine your goals as necessary. When circumstances change, your goals may need some changing. When you reach your first short-range goal, congratulate yourself and put another one in its place. Constantly refine and update your long-range goals. Try to be realistic. And remember, some goals are easier than others. But stay with this program. Before long, you will have the feeling of conquering the world.

A FINANCIAL STATEMENT

The next important block in building a strong future, preparing a financial statement, gives you both a knowledge of your financial position and a *direction* for your economic growth. You need to know your current financial numbers, even if they hurt, because knowing your monetary position can help you stay goal oriented.

The *first part* of a financial statement is a list of your *Assets* (what you own) and your *Liabilities* (what you owe). The questions on pages 28–30 are the guide for making these lists. When you have put down the numbers, done the additions, and subtracted the total of what you owe from what you own, you get your *net worth*. (The fact that Net Worth is in the liability column is an accounting formality—net worth is not in fact a liability.

Assets

Cash in banks $ _____

Cash in other institutions   _____

Collectible accounts receivable   _____

Stocks, bonds, and other securities
   (also list in Schedule B)   _____

Good notes receivable   _____

Cash surrender value of life insurance   _____

Automobile(s)   _____

Real estate (also list in Schedule A)   _____

Other assets (describe):

_____   _____

_____   _____

_____   _____

_____   _____

_____   _____

Total Assets $ _____

Liabilities

Notes payable $ _____

Accounts payable   _____

Taxes payable   _____

Contracts payable   _____

Real estate indebtedness
  (details in Schedule A)   _____

Other liabilities (describe):

_____   _____

_____   _____

_____   _____

_____   _____

_____   _____

Total Liabilities $ _____

Net Worth (Assets minus Liabilities) $ _____

Total Liabilities plus Net Worth $ _____

Some other information that can affect your financial position and your financial planning needs to be attached to the list of Assets and Liabilities. Some questions designed to develop this information are:

What assets in this statement are in joint tenancy?

ITEM	NAME AND RELATIONSHIP OF JOINT TENANT
_____	_____
_____	_____
_____	_____

Have you filed homestead? _____

Are you a guarantor on anyone's debt? _____ If so, give details:

_____

_____

Are any encumbered assets or debts secured except as indicated?

_____ If so, itemize by debt and security: _____

_____

_____

_____

Do you have business connections other than your employment:

_____ If so, state details: _____

_____

Are there any suits or judgments against you? _____

Are there any suits or judgments pending against you? _____

Have you gone through bankruptcy? _____

Have you made a will? _____

How many dependents have you other than your spouse? _____

The *second part* of your financial statement is another pair of lists, one of which is your annual *income* from all sources and the other your annual *expenditures* of all kinds. The lists on pages 31–33 are for your use in making up this part of your financial statement. Note that the list of expenditures does not include ordinary living expenses. Those will have to come out of your net cash income and you will need to make a fairly detailed list of them in connection with your cash-flow planning.

Annual Income

Salary or Salaries $ _____

Income from securities   _____

Income from rentals   _____

Other income (sources):

_____   _____

_____   _____

_____   _____

_____   _____

_____   _____
                                                       _____

Total Income $ _____

Less Total Expenditures   _____
                                                       _____

Net Cash Income   _____

Annual Expenditures

Real estate payments $ _____

Rent   _____

Income taxes   _____

Insurance premiums   _____

Property taxes   _____

Other expenses (itemize; include installment
    payments other than real estate; do not
    include ordinary living expenses):

_____   _____

_____   _____

_____   _____

_____   _____

_____   _____
                                          ══════════════

Total Expenditures $ _____

A cash-flow summary is sometimes considered a *third part* of a financial statement. Or it may be regarded as an annex or appendix to the minimum financial statement that consists of the asset-liability statement and the income-expenditure statement. In any case, you need to make up a cash-flow analysis for your own information in financial planning. It is discussed later in this chapter. Once you have prepared and analyzed your cash-flow statement, you may need to revise the expenditure list in your income-expenditure statement.

Schedules of certain assets are also needed as appendices to financial statements. One of these covers real estate and real-estate indebtedness; another covers such financial properties as stocks, bonds, and the like. Pages 33–35 provide guidelines for preparing them.

Schedule A—Real Estate

Location and Type of Improvement	Title in Name of	Estimated Value	Amount Owing	To Whom Payable
_____	_____	_____	_____	_____
_____	_____	_____	_____	_____
_____	_____	_____	_____	_____
_____	_____	_____	_____	_____
_____	_____	_____	_____	_____

Schedule B—Stocks, Bonds, and Other Securities

Number of Shares or Money Amount	Description	Current Market on Listed	Estimated Value on Unlisted
————	————	————	————
————	————	————	————
————	————	————	————
————	————	————	————
————	————	————	————

Another useful schedule covers your insurance policies, especially your life-insurance policies (their cash values are included in your list of assets). Your other insurance policies (health, accident, disaster, homeowner's) all have bearing on your financial planning. Knowing your needs and the amount of your protection against these risks is simply good business.

Insurance Schedule

On Life of	Company	Beneficiary	Amount
————	————	————	————
————	————	————	————
————	————	————	————
————	————	————	————
————	————	————	————

Automobile insurance:

   Public liability   Yes ____ No ____ $_____

Comprehensive personal liability

Yes ____ No ____ _____

Property damage   Yes ____ No ____ _____

Other coverage: _____ _____

Homeowner's insurance _____

Hospital-medical insurance:

On self _____

On spouse _____

On dependents _____

Personal accident insurance _____

How often should you prepare a new financial statement? I suggest that you do so at least once a year, but in any case do so when your financial condition changes, as it would change if you should sell some assets, make a significant capital gain, or take a significant loss. An up-to-date statement will tell you what you need to know about your financial growth.

CASH-FLOW ACCOUNTING

The purpose of accounting for your cash flow is to provide *control.* This accounting functions like the accelerator and brake combination on your automobile. If you have been spending too much (heavy foot on the accelerator) you will have to start slowing down and maybe even apply the brakes.

The important aspect is that accounting for cash flow gives you the knowledge of where your money is *actually* going. If you have been driving your money out of control for a while, then the rough treatment you have given your financial vehicle will make it difficult to pull it back onto the smooth road right away. To get it running smoothly again you may need a few financial tuneups.

If you have been weaving all over the financial highway, here are the tools for the first tune-up:

- You need to consolidate your debts, get a good grip on your spending practices, and start paying yourself first. What I mean by "paying yourself first" is that you take at least 10 percent of your earnings to work with. We will talk more of this later.

- You must put aside emergency money. (The "rainy day" fund.) The amount of emergency money to set aside is related to your specific situation. If you have a solid program of insurance and a job that carries good fringe benefits, including some protection against disability, you will need less emergency money than will someone with a more limited financial program. A good common-sense rule is to have three month's income set aside if you are well protected, nine to twelve month's income if you are not in a safe position.

- Study the examples of cash-control sheets on pages 37–40. The idea is to keep it simple and maintain cash-flow control. Notice the percent column. You should have an idea of what percent of your income goes toward mortgage payments, food, and other outlays. If the percent increases in any area you can immediately identify a problem before it gets out of control.

Cash-Flow Analysis—Income

SALARY AND TAKE-HOME PAY

Gross Pay		$_____
Withholdings related to taxes:		
Federal withholding	$ _____	
State withholding	_____	
FICA	_____	
State disability (if applicable)	_____	
Other	_____	
Deductions not related to taxes:		
Credit union	_____	
Life insurance	_____	
Medical insurance	_____	
Other	_____	
Total withholdings and deductions	$ _____	_____
Cash Available (Take-Home Pay)		$_____

ALL INCOME

Sources:
    Salaries (gross pay, from above) $ _____
    Bonus (before taxes)   _____
    Interest income (before taxes)   _____
    Dividend income (before taxes)   _____
    Capital gains (before taxes)   _____
    Other income (before taxes)   _____
                                                          _____
Gross income $ _____
Total withholdings and
        deductions from above   _____
                                                          _____
Cash available   _____

Cash-Flow Analysis—Reserve Funds

Current Period:
Cash available (from p. 37) $_____
Total spendable income
    requirements (from p. 40)   _____
                                                          _____
Balance of cash for reserves $_____

Available Reserves:
From current-period income $_____
Existing, carried forward from
    preceding period   _____
Gifts, etc., received in
    current period   _____
Inheritances received in
    current period   _____
                                                          _____
Total available reserves $_____

Use of Reserves:
Investments $ _____
Extraordinary purchases   _____
Set-aside for taxes
    not withheld   _____
Other   _____   _____
                                       _____   _____
Carried forward to next
    period (see Note) $_____

Note: Always leave the fixed amount you need for emergencies in *Reserves carried forward to next period.* This also applies to amounts in savings accounts, money funds, and any money put into the "holding pattern" for investment.

Cash-Flow Analysis—Spendable-Income Requirements

FIXED EXPENDITURES

Purpose	Planned Amount	Percent of total	Actual Amount	(+)/(−)	Percent of total
Mortgage or rent	$		$		
Taxes (other than withholding					
Installment debts (auto payments, etc.)					
Insurance premiums:					
Life					
Auto					
Homeowner's					
Health and other					
Total fixed expenditures	$		$		

VARIABLE EXPENDITURES

Food:					
Groceries	$		$		
Meals eaten out					
Fuel and utilities:					
Gas or oil					
Electricity					
Telephone					
Household operation:					
Improvements and repairs					
Other					
Automobile (fuel, oil, tires, maintenance)					
Public transportation					
Clothing:					
Mom					
Dad					
Children					

Purpose	Planned		Actual		
	Amount	Percent of total	Amount	(+)/(−)	Percent of total
Personal care	_____	_____	_____	_____	_____
Recreation, entertainment, vacation	_____	_____	_____	_____	_____
Medical and dental	_____	_____	_____	_____	_____
Miscellaneous	_____	_____	_____	_____	_____
Total variable expenditures	$_____	_____	$_____	_____	_____
Total fixed expenditures	$_____	_____	$_____	_____	_____
Total variable expenditures	_____	_____	_____	_____	_____
Total spendable-income requirements	$_____	_____	$_____	_____	_____

Once you get used to operating this way you will wonder how you ever survived without doing this.

The easiest method of keeping track is to use one of these sheets for each month and then summarize all 12 months on one master sheet at the end of the year.

Maybe you can have a better idea of your finances if you view your situation as if you were a corporation. Think of yourself as a small corporation of which you are the president, secretary, and treasurer, in which capacities you have to answer to the stock-holders—who, in this case, also are you. We know how stock-holders keep the presidents of corporations in line.

Every successful business uses the three basic financial tools we have discussed (the asset-liability statement, the income-expend-iture statement, and the cash-flow control sheets. You are the head of a business, and you must make well-controlled decisions as to how your money is spent every day. Once you get the whole system working, there will be a special satisfaction in getting your financial life back in order. The improvement will also open up new financial possibilities for you to explore.

Chapter 5 Where You Are Now— Introducing the Hayden Investment Chart

Now the time has come to start thinking about investments. If you could describe the ideal investment, what would it provide? Here are the most common responses to the question:

1. No risk.
2. Guarantee of principal.
3. Liquidity.
4. Inflation hedge.
5. Tax-free status.
6. Growth hedge.
7. Freedom from management.
8. High income.
9. Tax writeoff.
10. Convenience—it is easy to find.
11. Diversification.
12. Freedom from liability.
13. Recession hedge.
14. No money down!

Obviously there is no investment that encompasses all these criteria. That being the case, what is the next-best alternative?

Let's use an analogy. Suppose you are going to Dallas, Texas. (For those of you in Dallas, suppose you are going to San Francisco.) How would you plan to travel? How many modes of transportation would you use? Depending upon the distance from your home and

your reason for going, the forms of transportation could include an automobile, a bicycle, walking, a taxi, a commercial airline, a bus, a limousine, a motorcycle, a helicopter, a private airplane, and various others. The point is that you will end up using more than one mode of transportation and that the mode suitable for you may not be appropriate for someone else.

The same point applies to investments. You cannot have everything in one investment, so the best thing is to use several good investment vehicles to meet your goals and objectives.

Here are some guidelines to follow when you are looking into investments:

1. *What is the track record of the people managing the investment?* There are at least three approaches for checking a track record.

First, obtain all the information you can from the people offering or managing the investment. If it is the kind of investment you purchase and manage yourself, then you must investigate the economics of the investment itself. However, when someone is managing the investment for you, as in a limited partnership, the management will have a track record. Ask to have documentation about what they have done and how much money they have made for other people.

Second, talk to other people who have experience with the investment manager or general partner. These include investors and creditors, such as banks and savings and loan institutions.

Third, review the offering circular and prospectus. Because of the legal and technical language usually used in these circulars, they are very heavy reading. But much of the information is required by the various regulatory bodies (such as the Securities and Exchange Commission). It is good information and, even though the language may be hard to understand, it gives you a basis for asking for clarification on the important issues.

2. *Is there more demand than supply?* If few apartment complexes are being built, if the prices of homes are skyrocketing, and if mortgage money is tight, then the demand for existing apartments will probably increase. Until the supply can be increased, prices will probably go up. Likewise, if the supply of certain precious gems is being depleted and the demand is

increasing, they could be good investments. In other areas like energy and agriculture, demands have increased as supplies or availability have been decreasing.

3.   *What is the risk: low? medium? high?* Always remember that there is an element of risk in anything you can do with your money. If you rely on guarantees you must find out how strong the guarantee is. If the guarantor is a sound bank or the federal government, your principal is probably safe. I say *probably*, because in the event of total economic upheaval, even the banks or the state governments or the federal government may not be able to safeguard your principal. And even intact principal can suffer erosion from inflation and taxes; so can fixed return (like interest) from any investment. Hence the banks and the savings and loan companies invest some of their funds in areas such as businesses and real estate that have higher risk than the guaranteed investments they offer their own investors. The risk they take is well measured and provides opportunities for significant reward. I suggest you consider doing the same thing. But be careful never to take a risk from which you cannot bounce back if you should lose the money invested in it.

4.   *Are you lending your money with no chance for equity participation?* When you put money in a bank or in a savings and loan institution, you are lending money to them for a stated amount of interest. As you know by now, that probably means you are *losing purchasing power.* In order to experience true growth, you must exceed the inflation rate and neutralize the tax problem. In order to do that you must consider positioning your money in "things" and not in "accounts"—in the kinds of things that allow your money to grow as the investments increase in value.

5.   *How does the contemplated investment protect your buying power?* Though adequate growth can keep up your buying power, you should understand why—what the intrinsic value of the investment is that causes it to grow. What is it inside that investment that will help it to match or surpass the inflationary wastage?

6.   *Will you feel comfortable with the investment?* After several meeting I had with a gentleman in his sixties, he decided to reposition some of his money in three different investments. He had completed the necessary paperwork and written the checks. As he handed them to me, I noticed his hand was shaking

abnormally. When I asked him why, he said, "I know these are the right investments for me to make, but I've always kept my money in guaranteed savings and it's a little scary to me." While assuring him that it was a good idea to make the investments, I suggested that he not make them. After waiting a few weeks, he took a small step and made one investment. We waited a little longer to make the next investment so he could get the feel for how the first one worked. He gradually implemented his entire plan. The point is that no matter how good an investment might be, you should feel comfortable about your decisions. No investment is worth the high cost of emotional disturbance.

7. *Does the contemplated investment fit favorably into your tax situation?* Tax shelters can be injurious if not used properly. It is very easy to get off on a tangent when you are trying to beat Uncle Sam. Overkill in the tax-writeoff area almost always creates future problems. The advantage of a current-year tax saving can create a disadvantage in later years. A well-balanced common-sense approach used consistently can create a good tax advantage without unmanageable problems arising later. Only seldom should any investment be made for the tax benefit alone. It should be a good investment first, with a secondary benefit of creating some tax savings.

8.   *Are your preconceived ideas right about this investment?*
As a teenager at a circus, I remember seeing a large bull elephant
with a rope fastened to his hind leg and to a wooden stake that
had been driven into the ground. The elephant made no attempt
to get away. Why? He could easily have pulled the stake from the
ground and been free. The reason he didn't went back to when he
was a baby elephant; then, he had a very heavy chain fastened to
his leg and attached to a stake in the ground. No matter how hard
he tried, he could not free himself. Eventually his spirit was
broken. For the rest of his life he was convinced he could not pull
free. So he didn't try any more. *He had a preconceived idea.*

Many people have preconceived ideas like this, based on some
early conditioning in life. It may be important for you to take a
second look for the sake of your financial survival.

9.   *Does this investment seem suitably consistent with
some of your objectives?* Every investment you make should
meet one or more of your objectives.

10.   *Does this investment, when combined with your other
investments, help to meet all of your objectives?* In most cases, no
single investment alone will meet all of your objectives.

11.   *Is there enough diversification?* Your money can be
positioned so it will provide a hedge for both good and bad times.
Starting in the early 1970s before the recession of 1974 and 1975,
I suggested that most people own at least a small quantity of
silver and gold coins. My purpose was to provide insurance in
case of bad times and not even to consider these as an investment. This suggestion was and still is based on a rather
simplistic theory that if everything else was lost, the coins
would probably increase in value and provide capital for
recovery. Diversification will be determined by the kind of goals
you have. If you want growth, tax shelter, and a hedge for
inflation and recession, then you will probably need two or three
different kinds of investments.

THE HAYDEN INVESTMENT CHART

This chart will give you an overall look at all of your investments. It will give you a feel for your total situation. It is
illustrated on page 48. I use this format to teach clients how to
measure their investments in relation to their goals. I also have

taught this method to numerous planners throughout the country. It works. Here are the steps:

Step 1.   Across the top of the page list your investments; include a column for totals.

Step 2.   Fill in the amounts invested.

Step 3.   Put the percent of each investment in the next line. In the example, the $15,000 in savings is 37.50 percent of the $40,000 invested. The same for the rental house. The $10,000 in stocks is 25 percent of the $40,000. The columns must total 100.

Step 4.   List your investment criteria down the left side. This list will serve the twofold purpose of comparing an investment with your objectives and determining its suitability to your situation.

Step 5.   At this point put a *yes* or a *no* across from each one of your criteria and under each investment. In the spaces for Risk—Low, Medium, and High—put the percent for each investment (from Step 3). The answers I have provided in the example are the ones most often given in my classes and seminars. But yours might be different. All savings deposits are likely to be low in risk, for instance; rental houses or stocks might be medium or high in risk, or the house might be low. It is important that the answers be yours. If you cannot decide, then learn more about the investment.

Step 6.   You now have all the spaces filled in except for the column Percent Meeting Criterion. Start with the first criterion, Tax advantage. For each Yes, look back to the Percent of Total line to see what percent of total money invested it applies to, above the Yes. In this case it is 37.50 percent. Since that is the only Yes, put 37.50% in the last column (Percent Meeting Criterion) across from Tax advantage. Continue, doing the same for each criterion.

Step 7.   You now have a complete picture as to how your investments measure up to your investment goals. Do you have enough tax advantage? Compare this to the tax-planning format in Chapter 9 to see if it is consistent with your planning. Are you hedged enough for inflation? If you are more concerned about inflation than about recession, then you need a higher percentage of inflation hedge. Do you really need 62.50 percent liquidity, or can you meet your needs with 20 to 25 percent?

Maybe you might want to reposition some of these liquidity dollars to increase your inflation hedge? *You are now diagnosing your own problems.*

Step 8.   The next stage of planning is to look at other investment alternatives and decide what is suitable for you and is consistent with your goals. Based on these evaluations, you begin the process of deciding whether or not to reposition some of your assets.

The Hayden Investment Chart—An Example

	Savings	Rental House (Equity)	Four Stocks	Total
		Investments		
Amount	$15,000	$15,000	$10,000	$40,000
Percent of total	37.50	37.50	25	100

Criterion	Savings	Rental House (Equity)	Four Stocks	Percent Meeting Criterion
Risk { High			25%	25
Medium		37.50%		37.50
Low	37.50%			37.50
Tax advantage	No	Yes	No	37.50
Inflation hedge	No	Yes	No	37.50
Recession hedge	Yes	No	No	37.50
Freedom from management	Yes	No	No	37.50
Liquidity	Yes	No	Yes	62.50

Quite possibly you have been following the example and referring to it as you read the steps listed above. But you still need to make up your own investment chart. Take a look at your situation and prepare a set of columns for your investments and a set of lines for your criteria. Then fill in the spaces and compute the totals and the percents; filling the blanks may take some digging. Study the results carefully to see whether the investments really serve your objectives. Review the steps and follow them, especially step 7.

Also quite possibly, you are just starting out and have not yet made any investments. You may not yet have money to invest, or you may have uninvested money in a checking account or a low-return savings account. Then you can use the investment chart as a guide to formulating your investment program. If you are starting from the beginning, you need to concentrate first on a "starter" strategy—accumulating savings into a holding pattern. When you set aside enough in reserves for emergencies, then get ready to invest the next $1,000 you will soon have. Get your plan ready, and discuss it with your financial planner.

PART TWO MANAGING THE TAX BITE

Chapter 6 Income Taxes

WHAT IS YOUR TAX BRACKET?

Many people think that if you earn a taxable income of $30,000 and pay $6,238 in taxes, you are in 21-percent tax bracket. Not true. You did indeed pay just under 21 percent of your taxable income in taxes, but you are not in the 21-percent tax bracket—you are in the 37-percent tax bracket! Here is how it works.

Looking at the Federal Tax Rates for 1979, you can see that if you file a joint return you pay $6,201 on $29,900. On the last $100 that brings your income up to $30,000 you pay $37, or 37 percent. You always pay your highest taxes on the last taxable dollars of your income.

Tax on $30,000 Total Taxable Income

On $29,900 you pay taxes of	$6,201
On $100 you pay taxes at 37 percent	37
On $30,000 you pay	$6,238

You are in the 37-percent tax bracket with respect to that last $100 and you would be in the 37-percent bracket if your income were any amount between $29,901 and $35,200.

Be sure you subtract all your deductions and exemptions from your gross income to arrive at your taxable income. Some people inadvertently forget to do that and end up in a higher tax bracket than necessary.

TYPES OF TAXES

Ordinary Income Tax

We are all very familiar with this form of taxation. It applies to interest, dividends, rents, royalties, and commissions. It also applies to what is called personal-service income for the self-employed.

Tax on Short-Term Capital Gains

A short-term capital gain is the money received as gain or appreciation of any investment you sell within one year of the time it is purchased. The tax rate on it is the same as your normal tax-bracket rate on the gain received.

Example: An investment that cost $1,000 appreciates in ten months to $3,000.

$3,000	Proceeds of sale
−1,000	Invested
$2,000	Short-term capital gain (profit)
× .37	Your tax bracket (37 percent)
$ 740	The tax you pay

Tax on Long-Term Capital Gain

Long-term capital gain is the gain received from the sale of an asset held a year or more. You get a break because only 40 percent of the gain is taxable at your tax-bracket rate. It works in the following manner.

Example: An investment that cost $1,000 appreciates in 13 months to $3,000.

$3,000	Proceeds of sale
−1,000	Invested
$2,000	Long-term capital gain
× .40	The portion subject to taxation (40 percent)
$ 800	The amount subject to taxation
× .37	Your tax bracket (37 percent)
$ 296	The tax you pay
$ 740	Tax paid on short-term capital gain
− 296	Tax paid on long-term capital gain
$ 444	Tax savings

Federal Tax Rates on 1979 Income

MARRIED TAXPAYERS
FILING JOINT RETURNS

INCOME		TAXES	
Over—	But not over—		of the amount over—
	$ 3,400	-0-	
$ 3,400	$ 5,500	14%	$ 3,400
$ 5,500	$ 7,600	$ 294 + 16%	$ 5,500
$ 7,600	$ 11,900	$ 630 + 18%	$ 7,600
$ 11,900	$ 16,000	$ 1,404 + 21%	$ 11,900
$ 16,000	$ 20,200	$ 2,265 + 24%	$ 16,000
$ 20,200	$ 24,600	$ 3,273 + 28%	$ 20,200
$ 24,600	$ 29,900	$ 4,505 + 32%	$ 24,600
➤ $ 29,900	$ 35,200	$ 6,201 + 37%	$ 29,900
$ 35,200	$ 45,800	$ 8,162 + 43%	$ 35,200
$ 45,800	$ 60,000	$ 12,720 + 49%	$ 45,800
$ 60,000	$ 85,600	$ 19,678 + 54%	$ 60,000
$ 85,600	$109,400	$ 33,502 + 59%	$ 85,600
$109,400	$162,400	$ 47,544 + 64%	$109,400
$162,400	$215,400	$ 81,464 + 68%	$162,400
$215,400	....	$117,504 + 70%	$215,400

SINGLE TAXPAYERS

	$ 2,300	-0-	
$ 2,300	$ 3,400	14%	$ 2,300
$ 3,400	$ 4,400	$ 154 + 16%	$ 3,400
$ 4,400	$ 6,500	$ 314 + 18%	$ 4,400
$ 6,500	$ 8,500	$ 692 + 19%	$ 6,500
$ 8,500	$ 10,800	$ 1,072 + 21%	$ 8,500
$ 10,800	$ 12,900	$ 1,555 + 24%	$ 10,800
$ 12,900	$ 15,000	$ 2,059 + 26%	$ 12,900
$ 15,000	$ 18,200	$ 2,605 + 30%	$ 15,000
$ 18,200	$ 23,500	$ 3,565 + 34%	$ 18,200
$ 23,500	$ 28,800	$ 5,367 + 39%	$ 23,500
$ 28,800	$ 34,100	$ 7,434 + 44%	$ 28,800
$ 34,100	$ 41,500	$ 9,766 + 49%	$ 34,100
$ 41,500	$ 55,300	$13,392 + 55%	$ 41,500
$ 55,300	$ 81,800	$20,982 + 63%	$ 55,300
$ 81,800	$108,300	$37,677 + 68%	$ 81,800
$108,300	....	$55,697 + 70%	$108,300

ADD-ON MINIMUM TAX

An add-on minimum tax deals with gain arising from preferential items like stock options, specified accelerated depreciation, depletion allowances, and certain intangible drilling costs for gas and oil. The tax on these is fixed at a special rate of 15 percent of the gain. Since this tax is applied only to certain areas, your accountant should be made aware of any investment you make.

ALTERNATIVE MINIMUM TAX

The alternative minimum tax is payable only if it exceeds the sum of your regular income tax and the add-on minimum tax. The rates vary from 10 percent to 25 percent, but there is a $20,000 exemption. The rules are fairly complex, but a substantial long-term capital gain or a significant investment tax credit could trigger an alternative tax.

MAXIMUM TAX ON EARNED INCOME

Current tax law states that on the income you earn from salaries and personal service your tax bracket will be no higher than 50 percent. However, on the income from investments or "unearned" income (income your own labor did not create) you can be taxed to the maximum 70-percent bracket.

Tax planning can get complicated. It is very important to coordinate with your accountant before you make decisions that will affect your tax situation. Your financial planner will assist you in this process.

Chapter 7 **Tax Advantages**

THREE FORMS OF TAX ADVANTAGE

1. *Deferred Taxes.* Payment of the tax on current earnings postponed to a more advantageous time in the future.
2. *Tax-Free Income.* Income on which you pay no tax when received or in the future.
3. *Tax Writeoffs.* Real losses or bookkeeping losses (like depreciation) that reduce your taxable income. These do not necessarily mean a loss of profits.

DEFERRED TAXES

In the future you will probably be in a lower tax bracket. For most people this change occurs around the age of sixty, at retirement. For others, it can happen when they find themselves out of work, or if they decide to take time off without pay. You can take advantage of the situation.

One example of deferred taxes is the tax protection offered by the single-premium tax-deferred annuity. This new program is quite different from the traditional annuity with which you may be familiar.

Let us assume you deposit $10,000 in a single-premium tax-deferred annuity that is currently accumulating 7.5 percent interest compounded annually. In 10 years this will grow to $20,610 because you pay *no taxes on the interest* during those 10 years. If you deposit the same $10,000 at 7.5 percent in a savings account (likewise with interest compounded annually), and if you are in the 28-percent federal tax bracket, you will realize only 5.4

percent rather than 7.5 percent because of the taxes you will have
had to pay on the *interest as it is earned.* And in 10 years you will
have only $16,920.

Example:

$10,000, period 10 years, at 7.5 percent, tax deferred, accumulates to	$20,610
$10,000, period 10 years, at 7.5 percent, less tax paid each year, accumulates to	16,920
Additional deferred money	$ 3,690

That arithmetic means that at the end of 10 years, for every
$10,000 you set aside in the tax-deferred savings, you realize an
extra $3,690. You may say, "But I have to pay taxes on it some day."
True. But you have two advantageous elements working in your
favor.

1.   You will have that extra $3,690 working *for you* and there
will be more actual after-tax dollars left when you eventually
settle with the tax man. During this time the money stays under
your control, not the government's. A rule of thumb is that for
every dollar you can defer at 7.5 percent you will have an extra
dollar in 10 years.

2.   To take the earned interest out when you are in a lower tax
bracket, and pay the taxes on it then, is obviously to your
advantage. Moreover, if you take the money out a little at a time,
you will defer your taxes even longer, for you then pay taxes on the
money only as you use it. I will explain more about this type of
annuity in Chapter 9.

One disadvantage of deferring your taxes is that you probably
cannot use the *earnings* without initiating a tax.

TAX-FREE INCOME

"Tax free" means you do not pay taxes on the income—ever.
Interest on municipal bonds is one of the better examples of this
form of income. In recent years the interest rates on these bonds
have been between 5 percent and 7 percent, generally lower than

the interest rates on taxable-return investments. The value of this lower rate of return in your financial program depends on your income-tax bracket. It you are in a 50-percent tax bracket and the bond yield is 6 percent, that would be the equivalent of a 12-percent taxable return on an investment.

The disadvantages of municipal bonds are the lower yield and the possibility of the sale value going down. You might be forced to hold the bond until maturity or take a loss on the sale. Also, if you successfully reduce your income-tax bracket, the advantage of tax-free income may be significantly reduced.

TAX WRITEOFFS

A tax writeoff occurs when you are able to reduce the amount of your current year's taxable income as a result of allowable deductions. Many of these are bookkeeping losses only.

Mortgage payments present a good example of a tax writeoff. The part of each payment that reduces the principal of your mortgage is usually a very small segment of the total installment. The payment also includes a variety of other costs, but the largest portion goes to pay *tax-deductible* interest. This interest is a *tax writeoff*; therefore it lowers your taxable income.

Now look at the tax-writeoff worksheet that illustrates the advantage. Assuming a joint-return taxable income of $24,000, the federal tax would be $4,337. If mortgage payments are $500 a month, totaling $6,000 a year, the interest portion of the $6,000 could be $5,700 or 95 percent of the total paid. You would thus pay only about 5 percent or $300 toward the reduction of the balance of principal on the mortgage. The good part is that the $5,700 is a *tax writeoff*. By subtracting this $5,700 from your $24,000 taxable income, you will reduce that taxable income to $18,300. On that figure you will pay $2,817 in taxes instead of $4,337, creating a *tax saving* of $1,520. The net cost of the year's mortgage payments is therefore $4,480. The rest was effectively paid by the money that would otherwise have gone into taxes.

Interest on a mortgage is only one example of a tax writeoff. There are many others. For instance, a writeoff is often available in connection with investments in real estate, energy, agriculture, leasing, and research and development. Numerous investment vehicles will give tax writeoffs. In Part IV we will investigate several of these investment possibilities.

Tax Writeoff Work Sheet

Vehicle: Annual interest on home mortgage.

Tax without tax writeoff:
 1. Taxable income $24,000
 2. Tax due (28-percent tax bracket) $4,337

Tax with writeoff of interest:
 3. Total interest paid in year
    (95 percent of $6,000 mortgage payments)   5,700

 4. Net taxable income after interest deduction $18,300
 5. Tax due   2,817
 6. Net savings with tax writeoff $1,520

Amount invested (annual mortgage payment) $6,000
Less tax saved   1,520
Net cost of investment (mortgage payments) $4,480

Chapter 8 Government Tax Shelters

Certain tax shelters are designed by federal and state law to encourage you to plan for a solid retirement program. These shelter vehicles are extremely important. You should utilize them if your situation warrants. They are the safest kind of tax shelters. Basically, there are four:

1. Keogh Plans (HR 10). There are also mini-Keogh plans.
2. Individual Retirement Account Plans (IRA).
3. Tax-Sheltered Annuities (TSA).
4. Pension and Profit-Sharing Plans.

Here we will talk only about the fundamentals of each. The details you can work out with your planner/adviser. Incidentally, only earned income qualifies for these plans; passive income from investments does not qualify. However, income earned from investments inside one of these tax shelters is tax-deferred.

These tax shelters are examples of three basic money concepts: (1) tax writeoff; (2) tax deferral; (3) compounding. In each of the four tax-shelter plans the amount of money you put in is a 100-percent tax writeoff. That means you reduce your current taxable income by the entire amount you invest. Equally significant is the fact that you pay no current taxes on the earnings of the investments in the plan. They are *compounding* on a *tax-deferred* basis.

There is a great deal of confusion over these plans, because most people don't realize they are *vehicles* and *not investments* themselves. They're like empty boxcars, and in some cases you can load your tax-shelter boxcar with a mixture of investments. You don't have to put all your tax-sheltered money in savings or insurance or annuities. You can choose real estate, antiques, art, diamonds, leases, mutual funds, the stock market, Swiss francs, or a myriad of other things.

There are two methods of creating these plans. The first is to pick a product-oriented company that has prototype plans. Most insurance and mutual-fund companies, banks, and savings-and-loan firms have these plans available. The problem is that they generally require you to invest all or part of your money in their products—the investments they sell. Doing this may or may not give you the flexibility you want or need.

The second method is to pay a fee to an independent administrator and trustees and tell these people where to invest your money. Prototype plans are also available in this method.

Which method you choose will depend on how much you will eventually contribute to the plan and whether you can accomplish the goals you want to realize. The point is, *you run the plan— don't let the plan run you.*

KEOGH PLANS

1.   *Who can use a Keogh Plan?* The Keogh Plan is for the self-employed. Although you may be employed, if you work for yourself on the side you can put earnings from that self-employment into a Keogh Plan.

2.   *Do I have to include my employees?* Generally yes, after they have been with you for three years.

3.   *How much can I invest?* Up to 15 percent of earned income, or $7,500, whichever is less. There is an exception to this, in that it is possible to structure a defined-benefit plan. You stipulate what you want to retire on and a rather intricate formula is used to determine actuarially what amount you need to contribute in order to realize the monthly income you desire to have at the time of your retirement. In many cases, depending on your age, that method could permit you to contribute substantially more than $7,500.

4.   *When can I start taking money out?* When you are 59½ or older. Prior to that there are severe penalties.

5.   *Do I have to start taking money out when I reach 59½?* No, you can wait until you are 70½.

6.   *When is your money in a Keogh Plan taxed?* When you receive it as a distribution from the plan.

7.   *How is the money taxed when it is distributed?* As ordinary income and in some cases under special income-averaging rules.

8.   *Who designs the Keogh Plan?* The kinds of companies mentioned, or independent administrators and trustees.

9.   *What is a mini-Keogh Plan?* It allows you to put up to $750 a year into the plan regardless of how much you earn from self-employment.

INDIVIDUAL RETIREMENT ACCOUNTS (IRA)

1.   *Who can use an IRA?* Any working person, employed or self-employed, who is not covered by any other kind of retirement plan.

2.   *How much can I invest?* Fifteen percent of earned income or $1,500, whichever is less.

3.   *When can I take the money out?* At age 59½ or older; not sooner without severe penalties.

4.   *How is IRA money taxed?* As ordinary income plus special income-tax averaging rules.

5.   *When is IRA money taxed?* When you withdraw it.

6.   *Who designs an IRA?* Generally, the same companies that design Keogh Plans.

7.   *Can I include my spouse?* If your spouse is unemployed you may set up two separate IRAs and the deductible contribution is evenly divided between the two accounts to a maximum of $875 from each of you (total $1,750).

TAX-SHELTERED ANNUITIES

Tax-sheltered annuities are available to school teachers and to employees of nonprofit organizations. There is a rather intricate formula, but in *general* terms people in these categories can add a maximum of 20 percent of compensation for the taxable year in a tax-sheltered annuity. The investment actually amounts to a payroll reduction. There is a variety of products, but they fall into three main categories: variable annuities, fixed annuities, and mutual funds. Extreme caution needs to be exercised in choosing a TSA vehicle. An analysis needs to be made of the cost of getting into the investment as well as the cost of getting out of it. Some TSAs have no cost going in but charge on termination. Your financial planner can be of valuable assistance in helping you choose the proper vehicle.

PENSION AND PROFIT-SHARING PLANS

Pension and profit-sharing plans are created only for employees of corporations. The corporation contributes up to 25 percent of the employee's salary. There are special ways to make the contribution more. This kind of program definitely calls for planning by a specialist who has expert familiarity with these plans. You should be aware of the vesting schedules of these plans—in case you leave a job before retirement, you may be entitled to some money.

SUMMARY

The tax shelters mentioned in this chapter were described only sufficiently to give you a bare-bones idea of what they do. One very important benefit of some of these retirement plans is that proceeds will not be subject to estate taxes if paid to a named beneficiary over certain periods of time. This is another piece of the planning puzzle that your financial planner can identify and thereby provide you with assistance and direction.

Chapter 9 **Tax-Planning Strategy**

Tax planning is the use of all possible legal avenues to reduce your taxable income. It is best to plan two or three years ahead, using the best projections available.

The three *requirements* for sound tax planning are:

1. The ability to reposition some of the money you have accumulated.
2. The ability to save money each year.
3. The use of vehicles that are suitable to your situation and with which you feel comfortable.

These are the three phases of tax planning:

1. *Decide on Your Tax-planning Objective.* In doing so, first project your taxable income and your expected income taxes for the next three years. Once you have computed the total amount you *would* pay in taxes, your objective naturally is to reduce that amount, that is, find ways to pay less. Your situation may change, but you have made an effective plan and you can revise it. You may require nothing more than a course correction.

2. *Carefully Work through Your Own Figures on How to Reduce Your Taxable Income.* This is a conceptual exercise using certain assumptions like normal salary increases and the amount of writeoff that would result from repositioning some of your money into new investments.

3. *Then Evaluate Your Program as to How Close You Came to Your Objective.* This tax-planning strategy can be very effective. It works whether you have one thousand dollars or many thousands of dollars to invest. Remember, we are talking about tax avoidance, which is legal—not tax evasion. The difference between the two is a few years in prison, a heavy financial penalty, or both.

As I have shown in the following example, for phase 1 you project what you think your taxable income will be for the next three years. In the illustration I have assumed a raise each year which gives you a three-year total of $78,000 in taxable earnings. Remember these are taxable earnings *after deductions* and *exemptions* from gross income. The total tax bill would then be $14,883. And this is federal tax only. If you live in a state that taxes your income, the state taxes must be added.

Tax Planning—Phase 1

	First Year	Second Year	Third Year	Totals
Taxable income	$24,000	$26,000	$28,000	$78,000
Income tax (federal only)	4,337	4,953	5,593	14,883

Now, let us look at phase 2. Don't try to understand this chart all at once—take one year at a time. The concept is to create tax advantage mostly in the form of writeoff. We have made several assumptions, which are pointed out as we go along.

Tax Planning—Phase 2

	First Year	Second Year	Third Year
Amount repositioned (invested)	$10,000	$ 5,000	$ 5,000
Tax savings to be invested	–0–	+ 1,592	+ 1,717
Total invested	$10,000	$ 6,592	$ 6,717
Taxable income	$24,000	$26,000	$28,000
Tax writeoff from investment made the:			
First year	– 6,000 [a]	– 2,000 [b]	– 2,000 [b]
Second year		– 3,955 [c]	– 1,318 [d]
Third year			– 4,030 [e]
Adjusted taxable income	$18,000	$20,045	$20,652
Taxes:			
Original liability	$ 4,337	$ 4,953	$ 5,593
Adjusted liability	2,745	3,236	3,400
Tax savings	$ 1,592	$ 1,717	$ 2,193

[a] 60 percent of $10,000
[b] 20 percent of $10,000
[c] 60 percent of $6,592
[d] 20 percent of $6,592
[e] 60 percent of $6,717

At this point don't be concerned about investment selection.

Study the sample charts of phase 1 and phase 2 and then read the explanation of phase 2 that follows. Refer back to the chart from time to time to help your understanding. Do not be discouraged if you have trouble mastering the phase 2 chart and its explanation the first time through. It is new ground to most people.

The initial assumption is that there is a 60-percent writeoff the first year on the $10,000 invested. The writeoff in each of the next two years is 20 percent on the same $10,000. Over the three-year period you will write off 100 percent of the $10,000. Each new block of money invested (repositioned) will have the same assumption. I have further assumed you will invest the tax dollars that will be saved; doing this gives more strength to the plan. Later we will discuss the kinds of investment that result in tax writeoff. An example is an investment in real-estate partnership. The writeoff is created through depreciation and various expenses. These writeoffs are passed through to the partners as owners.

The first year of the plan there are no tax savings to invest, so your total investment is $10,000. The taxable income of $24,000 was already established in phase 1.

In the tax-writeoff section you put in the first year's writeoff, which is 60 percent of the investment or $6,000. Subtracting that from $24,000, you now have a taxable income of $18,000. Originally you would have paid $4,337 in taxes on $24,000; but now you will pay only $2,745 on an adjusted taxable income of $18,000. You save $1,592 in taxes the first year.

The second year, the assumption is that you will reposition $5,000 of the capital plus the $1,592 in tax savings from the previous year. Follow the same sequence as the first year's. You will notice that in the tax-writeoff line across from First year there is a minus $2,000; that is 20 percent of the original $10,000 invested the first year as a writeoff for the second year. The figure under that (–$3,955) is 60 percent of the $6,592 that was invested for the first time in the second year. Subtracting both these amounts from $26,000 makes the adjusted taxable income for the second year $20,045. The second year's savings is $1,717.

The same sequence applies to the third year. As you look at each line remember that the minus $1,318 is 20 percent of the $6,592 invested in the second year and that the minus $4,030 is 60 percent of the $6,717 invested in the third year.

Tax Planning—Phase 3, Summary

Amount of capital repositioned (invested)	$20,000
Amount of tax dollars saved	+ 5,502
Total amount	$25,502

TWO IMPORTANT RESULTS

First result: You repositioned $20,000 of capital and in addition you invested the tax savings of $5,502. You now have a total of $25,502 invested. Forgetting for a minute the tax savings of $5,502, how much *tax-free compounded return* (remember those terms) would you have to receive on $20,000 to have it grow to $25,502 in three years? The answer is about 8.5 percent a year. You just gained on the tax man and on inflation at the same time. *Moreover, we haven't figured in the return on the investment.* You were able to make that $5,502 *solely* by reemploying the tax dollars you saved through *tax writeoff.*

Second result: The original objective was to recover as much as possible of the $14,883 you normally would have paid in taxes for those years. You recovered $5,502. That's a 37-percent savings of the total original tax bill.

Recently, I received a call from one of my clients, who told me, "What a different feeling I have, as April 15 rolls around each year." He is employing the above strategy and successfully overcoming one of the main obstacles to building wealth: taxes. This reaction is repeated by several people each year. They are beginning to win the money game. Now you can do the same.

PART THREE **PROTECT YOURSELF PRUDENTLY**

Chapter 10 Life Insurance

Life insurance is a positive solution to the negative situation that someday you are going to die. Overcome the resistance to thinking about your death. You cannot cancel your departure by refusing to plan for that day. Develop your thinking to the point where you can honestly confront the issue. The whole idea is a negative and, as with so many other unpleasant aspects of life, you will be better off to confront the problem and solve it.

The cash value in life insurance should not be used as an *educational* or *retirement fund* or as a *savings vehicle* if you live. The main purpose of life insurance is to provide money in the event someone dies. For example, it *is* a purpose of life insurance to provide for your children's education if you die.

Some people feel a need for millions of dollars of coverage, while others think little or none is sufficient. The amount of coverage you need depends on many factors. Start thinking about how much protection you require.

The three main considerations in selecting your life insurance are: (1) needs, (2) kind of insurance, and (3) how you can pay the cost of insurance.

NEEDS

Decide how much insurance you need. You alone can determine what is best for you and your responsibilities. Here are a few of the needs you may have. The list is to be used as a guide. It will help you make up your mind as to your requirements. Each item will make up a portion of your total.

Personal Needs for Insurance

1. To cover a bank loan.
2. To pay a mortgage.
3. To provide income for your family.
4. To cover educational costs.
5. To pay other debts.

6. To cover costs of dying (funeral and medical bills).
7. To provide an emergency fund for a surviving spouse.
8. To pay estate taxes and other settlement costs.
9. To make a charitable gift.

Business Needs for Insurance

1. To provide the business with enough money to temporarily replace the economic loss of a key employee.
2. To provide cash for a buy-out agreement between partners.
3. To provide cash to buy shares of stock from a deceased stockholder's family.
4. To provide tax-deductible fringe benefits for employees.
5. To provide cash to pay off business loans and debts.

An Inventory of Needs

Make a list of the important needs and for each need write the dollar amount that is necessary to cover the cost of the item. For your planning purposes, consider the coverage to age 65 as temporary and any coverage to after 65 as long-term. Fill in the following:

Need for Money after Insured's Death	Amount Needed	
	Temporary	Long-Term
Total needs		

Now that you know the amount of money you require, you must decide whether to use your assets to pay for your needs or to cover them with insurance. For example, if you have $100,000 in needs and assets of $50,000, you may want to purchase $50,000 of life insurance to make up the difference. Or you may buy the entire $100,000 in life insurance. Buy why—if you already have $50,000 in assets? The $50,000 may be money you have in your home and you may not want your family to have to sell the home or refinance the property. Give this exercise some careful thought and deal with your needs realistically.

KINDS OF LIFE INSURANCE

Should you call a life-insurance agent and buy a policy? No—not quite yet. You need to know a little more about life insurance first. Your challenge in purchasing insurance is to decide which of various pretty packages is best for you. Insurance companies sometime wrap their coverage packages in exteriors that do not easily reveal the contents. Your challenge is to figure out what the companies have put into their package.

RED FLAG! *Program the following two guidelines into your mental computer.*

First guideline: Do not prepay premiums. Pay as little *now* as you can, because with inflation tomorrow's dollar will be worth less than today's, and you may as well spend the cheaper dollar for tomorrow's needs when tomorrow gets here. Prepaying premiums at today's dollar value will mean that you will pay more than you have to. Look at it this way:

The value of this year's dollar (whatever it is)	$1.00
Assume a 10 percent loss due to inflation	− .10
Purchasing power of next year's dollar	$ .90

Paying next year's premium with this year's dollar would cost you ten cents more in buying power than it would cost if you wait until the premium falls due. This concept applies to many "level-premium" policies. The reason they are level is that the premium is much higher the first year than it needs to be.

Second guideline: Pure life insurance has to cost you more every year of your life, for today you are closer to the day you will die than you were yesterday. Thus the older you get the higher the risk and the more the risk has to cost. Insurance companies have tables that indicate the chances you have of dying any given year

of your life. The companies know that a certain percent of people will die of natural or other causes during any specific year. And when you are 25 your chances of dying are much lower than they are when you are 65. As the company becomes more likely to have to pay off during increased-risk years, it will charge you more money to stay in the game. Your cost for life insurance goes up, therefore, for every birthday you have. The reason you may not know the cost goes up is that you may not recognize the growing price per thousand dollars of coverage. The prices are often hidden within the package disguised as something else. Learn to *read* the package.

There are three basic types of life insurance: (1) whole life (sometimes called ordinary life); (2) endowment; and (3) term. It may be an oversimplification to say that all life insurance is some form of term insurance, but that statement is not far from the truth.

WHOLE-LIFE INSURANCE

"Whole-life" means that you pay premiums during your entire life and have little more to show for them than having a forced-savings account. I am suggesting that you should know what you are buying.

If you buy a car, you should be aware of what extra accessories you get for the additional money you spend. The same is true with respect to insurance. You can be insurance-smart without knowing all about insurance. You need to know what protection you need and how to get the best buy.

There are several types of whole-life insurance, but they all have a savings component and a component of pure insurance. The policy is drawn to a projected age of approximately 100 years, at which time its cash value (savings component) would become equal to its face value. If you purchase the policy at age 40 and pay into it over the years, the component of pure insurance *goes down* while the cash value (savings component) goes up. When you die the policy pays out the *face value*, which is equal to the combination of *cash value* and *pure insurance*. This means of course that your own cash helped pay what the company owes.

Because the pure-insurance part of the combination is decreasing each year, the cost to you per thousand dollars of coverage is going up. You may not realize this, because you are paying a *level premium*.

During the first years of a whole-life policy you are paying substantially more than the actual cost of the insurance. In effect, you are prepaying some future premium by contributing to cash value. During the later years there is much less pure insurance, but the cost per thousand dollars of protection has increased sharply. You have prepaid (or overpaid) in advance, creating some financial reserve for the company. Since the cash value of the policy is increasing over the years and you have prepaid some of the premiums, the insurance company is providing less pure insurance.

If you have owned and paid the premium on a whole-life policy for several years (at least four), you probably have significant cash values. If you choose to keep your policy, don't leave the cash values in the policy during periods of high interest rates. Instead, borrow the money at an interest rate of somewhere between 5 percent and 8 percent, depending on the age of your policy. Your interest payments are tax deductible. Then place the money in an account bearing higher interest or in a money-market mutual fund. During periods of high interest rates these funds have paid over 17 percent. Investing in them is simply managing your money wisely.

Some whole-life insurance programs are called "paid-up whole life." The company increases the number of dollars in the premium package so that you have a policy *paid up* at age 65 (or at some other set age) and you have coverage after that age without paying any additional premiums.

But *remember*, if you have such a policy, that you will have already paid. For example, if you pay into a $10,000 paid-up-at-age-65 whole-life policy, you may have put $8,000 into the program to have an additional $2,000 of pure insurance. This is *very* expensive insurance, but the psychology of having paid-up insurance sells innumerable policies of this type.

Some insurance companies pay "dividends." These dividends are not like the dividends paid on a stock share. Insurance dividends are a return of an overcharge of your premiums. And they are not taxable, because the insurance company is only returning your money, money on which you have already paid income taxes.

ENDOWMENTS

Endowments are insurance policies that pay off at a set date. A 20-year $10,000 endowment policy will pay in 20 years. Until the date of the endowment payoff, the difference between the amount you have paid into the policy and the face value is a death benefit. Should you die before the conclusion date of the policy, the company would pay its face value. Consequently, the premiums for endowments are the highest for any insurance because of the relatively short pay-in period.

TERM INSURANCE

Term-insurance policies vary like the colors of the rainbow. For instance, you can buy term insurance that you renew each year for an increasing premium or you can get a policy that decreases in coverage each year until it falls to almost nothing or until you reach some such age as 100. During several recent years much creative thought by the insurance companies has gone into developing new kinds of term-insurance programs. As a product, term insurance is generally a better buy than the two other life-insurance forms because it is closer to pure insurance. Term insurance has no cash value. It provides risk protection, which is the real purpose of insurance.

One of the better coverage buys is a combination of term insurance and an annuity. These coupled together generally outperform whole-life insurance and are a much more efficient use of your money. Currently there is no tax on the interest in an annuity as it is earned; the tax is deferred to a future time when your tax bracket will probably be lower. You can take irregular withdrawals from the annuity to help pay your insurance premiums. You can withdraw your principal from an annuity and not have to declare it on your tax return. When you eventually withdraw interest you will have to declare it as taxable income.

The term-insurance/annuity program offers excellent flexibility. If you work with the cash values within a whole-life policy, you will alter the overall payoff characteristics of the policy. But in the term/annuity combination, the use of the cash in the annuity has no effect on your protection program.

DEPOSIT TERM INSURANCE

A popular innovation in the life insurance field is a modified-premium product often referred to as *deposit term* or *modified premium whole life*. These products usually operate on ten-year cycles. After the first ten years, you can normally: extend the program on a guaranteed basis in increments of ten years for a higher premium; or convert to decreasing term; or convert to annual renewable term; or possibly convert to some other policy that the insurance company may offer. A special feature of these products is that the first-year premium in each ten-year cycle is larger than the premium for each of the subsequent nine years.

The reason for the higher first-year premium is to encourage you to keep your policy in force. Companies lose money on policies discontinued in the first few years, and they normally structure premiums to include an amount to cover those losses. Since "deposit term" plans have the higher first-year premium, the premiums overall are lower to reward those who keep their policies in force.

Generally, "deposit term" policies have a cash value starting as early as the fifth year. This cash value increases until the end of the tenth year on a tax-free basis to an amount much greater than the higher first-year premium.

Shop around for the best buy in this form of insurance. Make certain you are paying the lowest possible premiums for this form of coverage. Costs differ within the industry. There are several variations of "deposit term" insurance.

Another kind of term insurance is *annual renewable*. Each year you pay an increasing premium that rises just as the risk of dying rises. Some people are bothered by the ever-increasing premiums. But these same people would be really shocked if they realized what was happening in some of the other forms of insurance. The point is that this is very low-cost insurance.

HOW YOU PAY THE COST OF INSURANCE

Here are several ways to pay life-insurance premiums:

1.   Pay your insurance premiums annually. This is the least expensive way. If you pay quarterly or monthly, the cost to the company of keeping records goes up and you will pay this increased administration expense. This rule does not apply when inflation is at a higher rate than the extra administration expense. Though you would be paying a higher cost, you would be paying it with less valuable dollars.

2.   You can have your children or your spouse own the policy with you making a gift to them of the money to pay the annual premium. This will keep the proceeds out of your estate. Your financial planner and your attorney can make the necessary arrangements.

3.   You can put the money into a trust fund and have the trust pay the premiums. This also may keep the proceeds out of your estate. The disadvantage is that you can lose control of the policy. However, if the trust is initiated properly, the proceeds will pay the estate settlement costs.

4.   If you have a corporation, you may want to consider group insurance. There are many different plans. You can solve the life-insurance problem by arranging a corporation plan with a company specializing in writing this type of policy. Temporary or permanent, the advantage is that the premium is totally tax-deductible by the corporation with little or no tax consequence to you. Generally, you are better off with a group-insurance plan.

5.   Your planning program may have generated some tax-free dollars. These may have come from tax writeoffs, tax-free bonds, or current tax-free income from an investment. Whatever the source, consider using the tax-free dollars to pay your premiums.

6. In many cases a married person should consider having his or her spouse own the policy and pay the premium from a separate checking account. There are no income-tax savings in this approach, but this arrangement could keep the proceeds out of your estate.

7. If you have more than one life-insurance policy, you are probably paying too much in premiums. Every life-insurance policy has what is called a *policy fee* that ranges from $20 to $30 each year. After analyzing your situation, you may want to

consolidate your life insurance into one new policy. There are many other points to consider before taking this step.

Look over these and other ideas with your financial planner. The idea, as always, is to *get the most for the least.*

A financial planner does not consider a policy from just one company. The planner must keep abreast of what is happening in the insurance world. Many insurance agents represent only one company and they should be avoided. As a consumer you want as many different choices as possible. At the very least you deserve more objectivity than a one-company agent can be expected to have.

Before leaving the subject of "life" insurance, here is a quotation from findings on *Life Insurance Marketing and Cost Disclosure* by the Congressional Subcommittee on Oversight and Investigations in August of 1978.

The Federal Trade Commission's tentative conclusions based on the Society of Actuaries data show that the 20-year average rate of return on the $100 billion or more in cash values held by life insurance companies is three percent or less.

We are persuaded that, even after taking income tax into account, many consumers could consistently achieve returns on safe, alternative investments that would be higher than those received from many whole-life policies. The significance in dollar terms to consumers is quite substantial. A 30 year old insurance purchaser who buys term and invests in a fund yielding a five percent rate of return after taxes will have 50 percent more accumulated when he retires at age 65 than if he buys a whole-life policy with a three percent yield.

Chapter 11 **Disability and Health Insurance**

DISABILITY INCOME INSURANCE

A lawyer client called me recently to say, "Vern, a good friend of mine just had a heart attack and may not be able to practice again. It has made me wonder if I have enough disability coverage." After checking his records I assured him that he was well covered. But the chances of becoming disabled in one's lifetime are startling. Unless you properly address and resolve this risk, you could suffer an economic death

Here's how to go about determining how much disability insurance you need:

Step 1. Measure your economic risk. If you couldn't work any more, what would you and your family need to live on? Generally you can obtain disability insurance up to 50 or 55 percent of your income. Be realistic about your needs. Include mortgage payments, car payments, gasoline, and everything else that draws down your cash.

Step 2. Find out what existing disability benefits are available to you. Many employing companies continue paying full salary for a period of time. Social Security may cover your disability. Your state may have a plan that covers you. Perhaps you are covered by workman's compensation. Calculate when the existing coverage expires. If it is good for three months, then a commercial policy would have to start your further coverage after 90 days. That timing is important because the premium is thereby less than it

would be if the personal commercial policy had to start paying in 30 or 60 days.

Step 3. Determine the best way to purchase additional coverage to make up the difference. Keep the following points in mind:

A. The policy you purchase should be guaranteed renewable and non-cancelable to at least age 65.

B. Estimate how long you can wait before the benefits start. The longer you can wait the less your premium will be. This wait is generally called the "elimination period."
C. Decide how long you want the benefits to last. Both accident and sickness should be covered to at least age 65.
D. Carefully examine the policy's definition of disability. Does it cover you for disability without respect to your specific occupation or does it state that as long as you can work at anything you will not be covered?
E. Does the policy provide overhead-expense insurance? This is needed for business and professional people who have to meet such ongoing costs as rent, secretary salary, and the like for a limited length of time. In most cases this requires a separate policy.
F. Residual benefit insurance is needed in the event that you should be disabled to the extent that you can work only part of each day. The insurance company will pay the difference. Coverage of this type is available for an indefinite period of time.

HEALTH INSURANCE

Recently I received a call from a minister. His health had been bad and he had incurred about $30,000 of medical bills. His small congregation had not covered him and his staff with medical insurance. With his modest salary, it would take him several years to pay his medical debts.

You really can't afford to be without medical insurance. Though medical costs have soared in recent years and insurance premiums along with them, consider the alternative.

There are two levels of coverage. The first level covers the basic medical costs. These include visits to the doctor's office, treatments, perhaps prescriptions, and similar specified charges. This type of coverage usually has a deductible clause.

The second level covers major medical expenses such as long-term treatment for serious illness, surgery, and the like. It is really intended to cover catastrophic demands. It is sometimes called disaster insurance.

Most employing companies have group-insurance plans. A high percentage of the population is covered by these plans. If you are

not covered by a group plan you should have individual coverage. This kind of coverage can be obtained from a Health Maintenance Organization (HMO) like the Kaiser Foundation on the West Coast or from one of the many commercial insurance companies that provide medical plans.

Chapter 12 Casualty Insurance

Casualty insurance covers your house, property, autos, and many kinds of personal liabilities. The story of a physician who was too busy to give much thought to his insurance points out how expensive carelessness can be.

He owned the building in which he and five other physicians practiced. He owned eight cars and three houses, one of which was a winter home in the ski country of Utah. It was from that ski home that burglars stole paintings and antiques valued at $200,000.

This physician's insurance premiums on all the items in his financial inventory cost him more than $8,000 a year, yet the paintings and antiques in that home were not covered. The agent who wrote the coverage informed the doctor afterward that a special rider would have been required to cover the loss of the items from the burglarized winter home. It is not enough to just have insurance. Knowing the kind and the extent of coverage is equally important. Not knowing cost the doctor $200,000 and the agent a client.

Remember that your needs for insurance change daily. The item you insured yesterday has changed, probably increased, in replacement cost by today. Your home purchased for $60,000 is worth twice that ten years later. If over the years you have let your fire insurance lag and your house is destroyed by fire, you may find that your coverage will amount to only a portion of your property's replacement costs. The rest will be out-of-pocket expenses for you to pay.

Insurance companies insure your home and possessions as if they were wearing out a little each day. The company will not pay

the replacement value of the insured items unless you have kept pace with their changing worth.

A financial planner could have pointed out the imbalance in the physician's homeowner's insurance coverage.

Another area where many people are not adequately covered is their car insurance. The minimum coverage that most states require is woefully inadequate. Your bodily-injury protection should be at least $100,000 on each person and a total of $300,000 for each occurrence. Property-damage liability insurance should be at least $100,000 for each occurrence. You should also include comprehensive and collision coverage, each with a deductible (the amount you pay) of about $100. The deductible amount really depends on your financial situation; the more you are willing to accept, the lower the premium. It is also wise to include uninsured-motorist and medical payments.

It is extremely important that your financial-planning team include an expert in casualty insurance. Most of your risks—fire, theft, accident, and others—can be covered by a good casualty company. I have an expert review each of my clients' insurance programs to make sure that they have adequate and complete coverage.

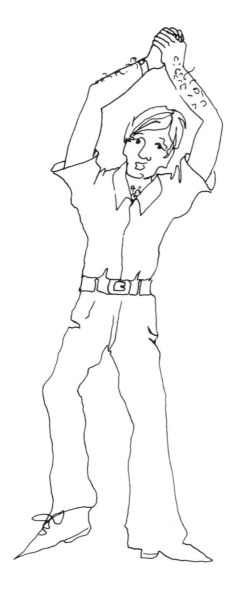

PART FOUR **USE YOUR MONEY AND PROSPER**

Chapter 13 The Use of Credit

Credit is very important in the financial world. Use it well and you increase your leverage in many ways.

YOUR CREDIT RATING

In theory you can have credit when a lender determines that you are responsible with money and have the ability to pay back the amount loaned and the interest within a period of time that is agreeable to both parties. Lending institutions have access to computer information on your past financial performances. If you have any bad marks they can cause you serious problems. The local credit bureau can often have erroneous information in your file.

By law, you are entitled to see your file at the credit bureau. You should check your own record. During a check on a client's file, we noticed that he was listed as having defaulted on a loan from a bank with which, he informed me, he had never done business. After he proved his case, the bureau removed the information from his record. It would still be there if I had not suggested he check his credit record. Needless to say, he now makes sure to check his credit status every year. You can clear your record at the credit bureau by taking proper documentation on the matter in question to the bureau for their inclusion in your file.

There are several ways to borrow money. You can get a loan on your signature without collateral. A loan of this type usually is not available unless you have a strong relationship with your bank and have proven credit worthiness.

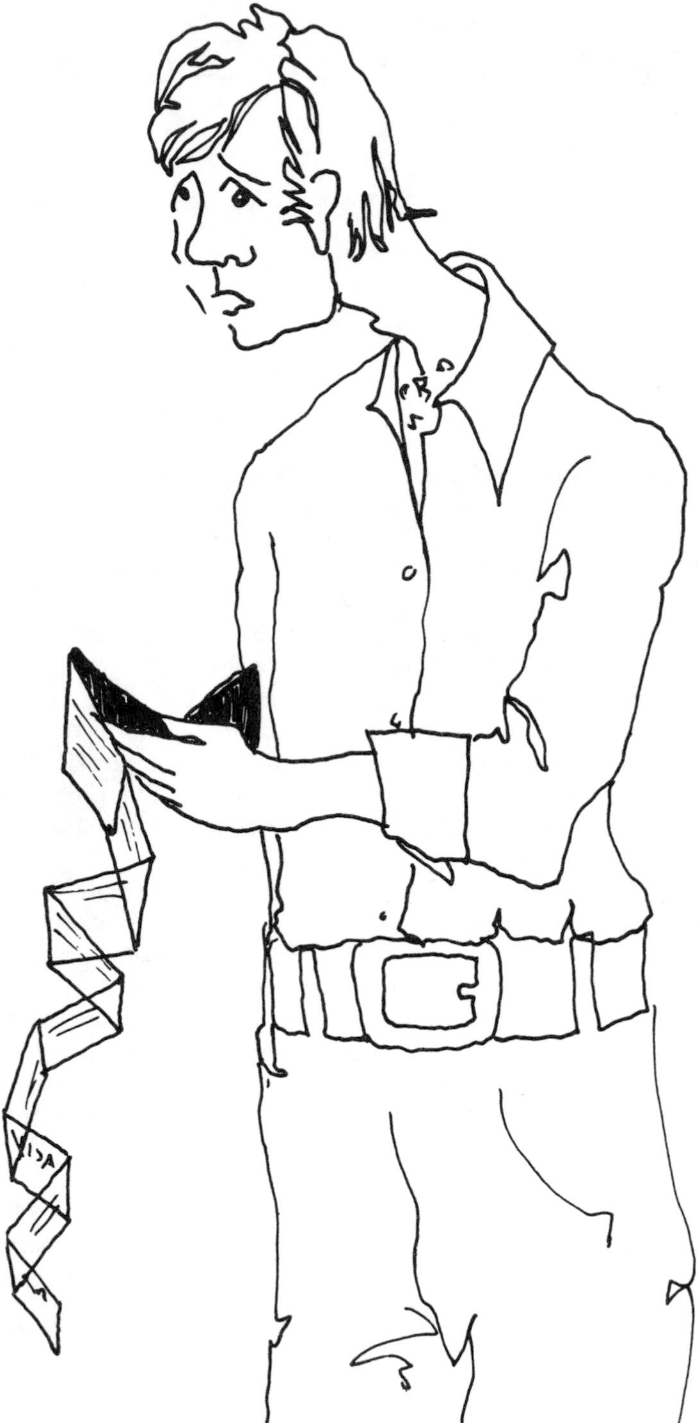
VIDA

When you have collateral to back up your loan, the bank may make a loan it would otherwise refuse because it can use the assets you offer to cover the loan. Collateral can be stocks or bonds or real estate or other commodities of value.

The most important information required to obtain a loan from a lending institution is your net worth, current income, and credit rating. Of these, the most important consideration in securing a loan, assuming you have a normal financial history, is your income. It is hard to borrow money with little or no regular income. The lending-institution people therefore ask you to fill out a financial statement. (See Chapter 4.) They also request your last two or three years' tax returns, and they obtain a retail credit report on you. If these items prove your ability to repay the loan, you will generally get it.

CREDIT CARDS

Credit cards have two potentials: *destructive* and *constructive.*

The most damaging obstacle to good financial planning is the abuse of credit. Our plastic society is credit-card happy and the cost is staggering.

I cannot recall when I last bought anything in a store that cost more than a few dollars and was not asked, "Will this be a charge?" To the stores that have them, the revolving charge account is a major source of income. Some large stores make more on their credit charges than they do on the actual sale of their products. That tells us how many dollars are being spent to borrow more dollars rather than pay for goods and services.

Several years ago a hard-working, high-living executive in New York City was charging every purchase for business and pleasure on his credit cards. He ran up debts of more than $50,000. When his business fell off abruptly and there was nowhere to go but into bankruptcy, he paid off his debts the hard way—he jumped out of a high window. There are easier alternatives for clearing up one's financial life. Hopefully, you're not in a jam as bad as his.

The answer to staying out of credit-card trouble is to maintain *discipline.* Your life can be consumed by credit cards if you don't keep a strong hand on your pocket plastic. If you are quick to use a credit card, stop and realize that using it is spending money. In many cases it is spending *more money,* because you pay interest on top of the purchase price. Doing that can get expensive. Maintain discipline on your credit purchases. Be as careful with your credit cards as you are with your cash. You are the only person who can prevent the misuse of your credit. Discipline—repeat—is most important.

Constructive credit is what you use when you have a credit card or two and never make a late payment. Because paying on time saves you money in finance charges, a credit card can provide a few weeks' interest-free use of money while, at the same time, furnishing you with an excellent record of your transactions.

Having a credit card *for your business* should be exactly that. Have a card in your business name and keep your personal charges separate. Carry another card for your private use.

Credit can be extremely useful. Use it properly and you will profit well.

Chapter 14 **Should I Refinance?**

The equity in your house is the difference between what you owe on your mortgage and what you would get if you sold the property. With the rapid growth of property values during the 1970s, the equity in most properties doubled or even tripled. Because of this increase, more and more people are asking the question, "Should I refinance?"

As an example: In Marin County, California, property values rose about 24 percent each year during 1977-1979. Property values

may not have risen as fast in other parts of the country, but they have gone up at an accelerated rate everywhere. This rise is an aspect of inflation.

Freeing some or all of the equity in your home for other investments can be a sound financial move. However, like all financial decisions, it should be approached carefully and with as much significant information as is available. A financial planner can be most helpful in this area, because his training enables him to have an objective view. Also he will have access to most if not all the "outside" information that you might need.

Now let us develop the "inside" information. Use the Financial Profile questionnaire. Answer the questions in the spaces provided. Make any notes that you might need in the margins.

Financial Profile

Your age _____ Your spouse's age _____

Your tax bracket (combined incomes) _____

How long do you expect to be in this tax bracket? _____

How solid is your employment/income situation? _____

How long can you count on the security of your employment?_____

_____

How long do you plan on living in your home? _____

What would be the interest rate on a new first or second mortgage? _____

What is the net worth of your assets other than your home? _____

_____

How much are your liquid assets worth? _____

How close to retirement are you? _____

What will your income situation be after retirement? _____

How much extra cash flow do you have? _____

How much additional mortgage payment could you afford to make? _____

Do you want your mortgage paid off by the time you retire? _____

What would you do with the money you would receive from refinancing? __

How much tax writeoff could you get from the refinancing money you would

receive and then invest? _____

What is a reasonable return you would expect from the reinvested funds?

What is the current balance on your mortgage? _____

Does your mortgage have any prepayment penalty? _____

What is your current monthly mortgage payment? _____

The answers to the Financial Profile questions will help you to make a decision as to whether or not you should pull some or all of the equity out of your home.

Recently, some clients of mine explored refinancing. We can follow them through the procedure.

They were in their early forties and made a combined income of $45,000. After deductions and exemptions, including the interest on the mortgage, they paid taxes on about $34,000. That put them into a 37-percent federal tax bracket. Their employment picture was stable with increases expected at reasonable intervals. They planned on remaining in the same home for at least seven more years. Their goals were to build their assets, taking medium risks while lowering their tax liability.

The market value of their home was $105,000, with a remaining mortgage of $30,000 at 8½ percent. The difference gave them an equity of $75,000. Their monthly mortgage payments were about $500. They had no prepayment penalty. They felt that their cash flow would permit an increase of $250 in the monthly mortgage payments. Thus, they could increase their refinanced mortgage payment to a total of $750 a month. Their big question was *should they refinance?*

Many personal considerations are involved in making a decision of this type. Every set of circumstances is different and you should not necessarily apply their guidelines to your situation.

My clients decided to refinance their home, taking a new $75,000 first mortgage at 10 percent to run 30 years. This required monthly payments of $653. They retained about $30,000 equity in their home. (It is generally not advisable to refinance to the limit.) They had decided to keep their monthly payment about $100 below what they thought they could afford. Now let us examine the points that produced their decision.

Their previous mortgage payment amounted to $6,000 a year, of which $5,200 was tax-deductible interest. Without this deduction they would have paid taxes on $39,200.

Taxable income before interest deduction	$39,200
Tax-deductible interest	− 5,200
Adjusted taxable income	$34,000
Federal taxes on $39,200 are about	$ 9,882
Federal taxes on $34,000 are about	7,718
Tax savings	$ 2,164

Subtracting the $2,164 from $6,000 yearly mortgage payments amounts to a net after-tax mortgage cost of $3,836 a year.

The new mortgage payments are $653 a month or $7,836 a year. Of that amount about $7,500 is deductible interest. Now instead of deducting $5,200, we deduct $7,500.

Taxable income before interest deduction		$39,200
Tax-deductible interest		− 7,500
Adjusted taxable income		$31,700
Federal taxes on $31,700 are about		$ 6,867

Subtracting the taxes paid ($6,867) with the new mortgage from the taxes paid ($7,718) with the old schedule shows that the new mortgage results in an additional tax savings of $851. Adding this to the $2,164 makes a total of $3,015.

The net after-tax mortgage payment under the new plan is:

	Per Year	Per Month
Total payments	$7,836	$653
Tax savings	−3,015	−251
Net payments	$4,281	$402

The total payments figure is well under the $750 that my clients felt they could afford. Hence they look fine with respect to cash flow.

The next question was how they should invest the $45,000 freed from the equity. We reviewed many options and possibilities. Their goals were to create tax savings, achieve growth with low to medium risk, preserve some liquidity, and maintain a hedge against inflation and recession. Based on research and their situation, they chose to position the $45,000 in four different financial vehicles. My Hayden Investment Chart helped them to determine the kind of investments they would use.

The projected seven-year results would be as follows:

The $45,000 was projected to increase to at least $90,000 from the accumulated return on investments.

The investments would yield an additional $6,000 in tax savings, which when reinvested should increase to at least another $10,000.

The total money value of the clients' investments in seven years would be about $100,000.

As a comparison, let us look at what might have happened if the clients had not refinanced and had sold their home after seven years. We have no way of knowing, but let us assume that the home increases in value by 10 percent each year. In seven years the home would be worth $205,000 and the balance of the mortgage would be around $21,000.

The sale price would be	$205,000
Mortgage (without refinancing)	– 21,000
Balance after sale (without refinancing)	$184,000

The new $75,000 mortgage in seven years would have been reduced to $71,000.

The sale price would be	$205,000
Mortgage (refinanced)	– 71,000
Balance after sale (with refinancing)	$134,000

Hayden Investment Chart

	Investments				
	Money-Market Fund	Second Deed (Mortgage)	Real Estate	Cable Television	Totals
Amount	$10,000	$5,000	$15,000	$15,000	$45,000
Percent of total	22.22	11.11	33.33	33.33	99.99

Criterion					Percent Meeting Criterion
Risk { Medium			33.33%	33.33%	66.66
Risk { Low	22.22%	11.11%			33.33
Tax advantage	No	No	Yes	Yes	66.66
Growth hedge	No	No	Yes	Yes	66.66
Inflation hedge	No	No	Yes	Yes	66.66
Recession hedge	Yes	Yes	No	Yes	66.66
Liquidity	Yes	½	No	No	27.68

Adding the values of the investments of the released equity ($100,000) to this balance-after-sale figure gives $234,000 as the total assets of my clients seven years after the refinancing.

Without the refinancing and investment, the total assets would be only $184,000—that is, the balance remaining after selling the house and paying off the old mortgage.

Total assets with refinancing	$234,000
Total assets without refinancing	184,000
Gain achieved by refinancing and investing released equity	$ 50,000

Chapter 15 **Investing**

There are literally thousands of investments. Taking your money out of a savings institution and placing it in "another" holding pattern will not be an effective use of it. You need to select an investment that meets your objectives with a relatively clear understanding of what you stand to gain or lose.

Some people go wrong by wanting to put their money only into a sure thing. The only sure thing is that in banks and other institutions with low rates of return your *buying power* will evaporate. Obtaining as much information as possible about an investment and diversifying your investment vehicles are probably as close as anyone can come to attaining a sure thing. Putting all your eggs in one basket is a well-known blunder.

Other people go wrong by feeling that they must have undivided ownership of what they invest in. Often, however, you will have *less* worry and *more* money if you own a piece of the action while someone else, who is an expert in the field, is making the mangement decisions. The choice is like deciding whether you are going to pilot your own airplane or buy a ticket on a commercial airline using highly experienced pilots.

LIMITED PARTNERSHIPS

Limited partnerships are one way of investing that allows you to diversify your dollars into several areas without requiring a huge commitment or attention to decision making. You are letting someone else be the pilot.

A group of people who agree to pool their money for investments and then hire an expert to acquire, manage, and eventually

sell the assets are known as limited partners. The limited partner
is generally not legally liable for more than what he or she has
contributed to the total purchase price of the investment. A
limited partnership includes a general partner (GP) who has the
know-how in the field of the particular investment. The GP
usually has some financial interest, but also participates in the
profits as reward for his managerial knowledge. He is legally
responsible for the proper operation of the investment.

If the GP is taking a lot of money up front, watch out! This is a sign that the GP may try to make his money early, turn his back on the investment, and not worry about achieving a strong profit at the time the investment is sold. The standard return for the GP is a share in the profit at the time of sale (along with the rest of the partners), rather than excessive fees and profits taken during the life of the partnership. Most of the tax benefits are passed on to the limited partners; in this respect, among others, limited partnerships differ from holdings of corporate stocks.

Some examples of limited partnership investments are discussed below.

ENERGY: OIL AND GAS

There are three kinds of oil and gas investments.

The *first* is *exploratory drilling.* Sometimes this is called wildcatting. It is very risky. If you don't play the long shots, stay away from this. You really should be worth a substantial amount of money to try it. The industry may bring in one or two wells out of every ten they drill. Some drillers may not do that well. If you are in a high tax bracket—at least 50 percent—your risk is reduced because you can write off approximately 100 percent of your investment over the first two years. In a limited partnership, you are required to qualify for the investment on the basis of net worth, tax bracket, and income. The requirements are determined by the Securities and Exchange Commission, the states' departments of corporations, and other regulatory bodies.

The *second* is called *development drilling.* This is much less risky than exploratory drilling. There are already producing wells in the general area to be drilled. The standard is about six to seven successes out of each ten drillings. And the writeoff is 70 to 80 percent of your investment the first year with the balance over the next year. As oil and gas prices continue to rise, the investment should be an excellent inflation hedge. Because of the demand outstripping the supply, it is also a good recession hedge.

The *third way* is to invest in oil and gas for *income.* There are companies that specialize in purchasing producing oil wells, buying the existing wells at bargain prices. These are sometimes offered for sale because the original developer wants cash to drill more wells. These wells generally have produced for at least three years. It is normal to get three appraisals on the wells before a partnership purchases them. A bank, an independent appraiser, and a geologist representing the general partner all submit their appraisals on the wells. Based on these evaluations, the general partner will make a decision whether or not to acquire the existing wells. The income is paid to the investors as long as the wells continue to pump—usually 15 to 20 years. There is a low writeoff of 7 to 8 percent of what was invested. However, a substantial portion of the income is tax-sheltered. And since the price of energy will continue to rise, this investment becomes a strong

inflation hedge. It is also a good recession hedge because of the tremendous demand regardless of the state of the economy.

Unless you are already wealthy, the only way you can participate in an oil-and-gas investment is through a limited partnership. There are partnerships with very acceptable track records in all three categories. The key consideration, once again, is "What is the most suitable for *my* situation?"

Some partnerships combine exploratory drilling with developmental drilling. In these, you get a shot at the big returns without taking as much risk as in wildcatting alone.

The best advice I can give is to consider investing a little money in two or three partnerships, rather than all the money in one. This technique increases the spread of the risk. Work closely with your financial planner in examining the record and the overall evaluation of the partnerships, and you will reduce the risk even further.

You need a minimum of $3,000 to $5,000 to obtain entry into most partnerships. Do not expect to make a killing. But a successful partnership will create good tax advantage and a respectable return for 15 to 20 years. Remember that most of these partnerships are not liquid—you cannot easily sell your share in the partnership.

AGRICULTURE

So you like to eat! So do the other 4 billion or so people in the world. And by the year 2010 there will be 6 billion mouths to feed! Every year there is less agricultural land to feed more people. The supply/demand relationship is critical to this kind of investment. The less of any good nutritional crop, the higher the price goes. The secret of making a profitable investment is to project the demand for a crop to some point in the future so you will be on the right side of demand. There are four basic elements to a good agricultural investment.

First: Good management. The general partner's management team must include successful farmers or you should keep out. Local farming experience is also helpful. It is always easier to do business with a trusted farmer who is well known in the area.

Second: Value of the farm land. Good farm land has appreciated rapidly in recent years. That appreciation is where the profits ultimately lie. In the period 1975-1979 the demand for farm land has pushed values up an average of 25 percent a year. This large increase is the direct result of the need for food throughout the world, combined with continuing inflation and the declining value of the dollar in international money markets.

Third: Timing. Timing is an important skill for the management team. Those factors that can be controlled, such as cultivation, fertilization, irrigation, and harvesting, must be executed with precision because the uncontrollable factors such as weather and market conditions often do not allow margins for error.

Fourth: Diversification. There are two general categories of crops: permanent crops and temporary or row crops. Permanent crops are those like apples, oranges, figs, grapes, and walnuts. Temporary or row crops are cotton, wheat, sorghum, tomatoes, beans, and such.

There are numerous strategies of creating agricultural profits using different combinations of crops. The key will be the ability of your management team. An excellent combination would be a mix of permanent and row crops. Diversification reduces risk. Row crops have the potential of creating more rapid cash flow; permanent crops may take four or five years before any cash flow is created.

There is potential for excellent tax writeoffs and tax sheltered income from farm investments. It really depends upon which particular investment you are in.

Again, the limited partnership is the most practical approach for you to consider. For $3,000 to $5,000 minimum, you can pool your money with others and let the experts till the ground for you. As with most partnerships, you cannot cash in at just any time you want, so be prepared to leave your money in for a few years.

CABLE TELEVISION

One of the fastest-growing and most profitable industries in North America today is cable television. The development of this industry is likely to be one of the most significant socio-economic events of the 1980s.

The cable television industry added 2.5 million new subscribers during the three-year period of the 1973-1975 recession. A recent article in a national magazine points out that cable television at the time of publication was reaching about one person out of every

five in the national television audience or about 14.5 million out
of 73 million television households. At the present rate of growth,
one out of every three households will have cable television by the
end of 1981.

Here are some reasons for a probable continuing growth of cable
television:

A. System saturation (expansion; more homes per block)
B. System extension (new housing areas; mobile-home parks)
C. Rate increase (for example, an increase from $6 to $7 per
   month per subscriber is a 16.6-percent increase)
D. Favorable legislation
E. Service expansion possibilities
   1. Motion pictures (Home Box Office for example)

2. Home security systems (fire and burglar alarms; "panic buttons")
3. Two-way medical services
4. Political communication (City council meetings, for example, can give the subscriber the capability to push buttons to give responses to issues. The mayor of Columbus, Ohio, did this in 1978.)
5. Talent shows (viewers can register approval or disapproval)

Here is a list of attractive features of investment in cable television:

A. Little accounts-receivable problem. If people fail to pay, they simply get cut off.
B. Little inventory problem.
C. A broad revenue base. One or two disconnects have little impact on the return from the investments.
D. Recession hedge. During hard times, cable television is the cheapest form of entertainment.
E. Inflation hedge. A cable television system is a good inflation

hedge because each newly established household is a prospective customer for the service. In addition, a cable system can sell more services to existing subscribers as well as increase its basic fees to offset inflation.

F. Limited consumer access. Each system has what amounts to a monopoly in its area franchise.
G. A relatively short holding period (three to five years).
H. Tax benefits

There are two ways to invest in cable television: stock ownership and partnerships. The partnership approach can pass on significant tax advantages that are not available to the stock purchaser. Your participation in a partnership is more direct than it can be in a stock company. An example of a stock company would be Warner Brothers Communications, a rapidly expanding operation. An example of a company that specializes in public partnerships is Jones Intercable in Denver, Colorado. Jones has not only done an excellent job acquiring and managing cable television systems, but is also the first to provide public partnerships.

To invest in a partnership you would need a minimum of $2,500. And you would, of course, try to make sure it is a suitable investment for your situation.

BUDGET MOTELS

It is hard to find an inexpensive place to sleep when you are on the road. There has been a blind spot in the development of motels. Up to now you have had to choose between an inexpensive motel with virtually no amenities or an expensive one with more extras than you need for a night's rest.

Budget motels are filling that gap. They offer a few amenities like in-room television but charge 20 to 25 percent less than the well-known national motel chains. They have very carefully defined their market and developed in strategic locations.

The motel business is always risky. To help reduce risk, the new motels whenever possible are built near airports. The general partners pay cash for the land and construction. This financing increases the cash flow because there is no mortgage payment. When the motel has been seasoned for four or five years, the partnership mortgages the property for about 50 percent of its value (which with inflation has probably increased substantially) and builds another motel. The objective is to sell the motel in about eight to ten years for a good profit. For about $3,000 it is possible to get into a partnership. It is not a liquid investment, so plan on staying with it.

MINI-STORAGE AREAS

Many people don't have a basement or garage large enough to hold all of their excess goods. The solution is to rent some inexpensive space and store them. Many businesses do the same thing in order to save money.

Many mini-storage sites are built with all cash, then leveraged with financing, and eventually sold off. The idea is to get your investment back through cash flow; then, when the facility is mortgaged, to get your cash back again; and then to hold on until the operation is sold. Some operations are doing very well, but mini-storage is still a relatively new endeavor and has not yet gone full cycle. The primary problem to watch for is oversaturation in any given area.

Mini-storage areas are a good hedge for inflation and to a lesser degree a hedge for recessions. They are not liquid, but they offer good potential cash flow and long-range profits. You can get into a limited partnership for about $3,000.

REAL ESTATE

Because of the boom in real estate for the last few years, many people feel that all they have to do is own some and they will get rich. There has been an almost panic fervor to buy houses, duplexes, four-plexes, and small apartment buildings. In the late 1970s people would line up at new housing tracts in Southern California and buy out the entire tract in one or two days. Developers in Hawaii would hold a cocktail party and sell out a whole new condominium complex. During 1976-1979 the price of houses in Marin County, California, rose at the rate of 24 percent a year.

Some people bought houses as an investment despite sizeable negative cash flow. That means that though they were able to scrape enough money together to make a minimal down payment on a piece of property, they had to make monthly payments for both a first mortgage and a second mortgage. And even with a tenant paying rent on their investment house, these owners still had to pay from $100 to $400 a month over income to meet mortgage payments. The problem in this situation is that a combination of events could cause them to lose their investment and the hard-earned money that they put into it. How could it happen? Through any one or a combination of the following:

A. The tenant moves out or for some reason cannot pay the rent.
B. The owner (or one of the owners) becomes unemployed and cannot carry the burden of the excessive mortgage payments.
C. The owner cannot sell because interest rates went up on new financing.
D. Fewer buyers can qualify for a loan.
E. Lending institutions stop loaning money unless the owner occupies the house.
F. Fewer people can afford to pay the inflated price for the house.
G. The market goes into a downswing.

The rational investor does things differently. He or she scouts around for good buys and always makes sure the financing is right so there is little or no negative cash flow. He or she is selective in choosing a good tenant. The property is enhanced by improving some of the cosmetics.

Don't look for rapid turnovers—the fast-buck deals. Build on gradual consistent acquisition of reasonably priced properties.

A lot of wealth has been accumulated in real estate. It will continue to be possible for the wise and cautious investor to gain it. There are basically two ways to invest in real estate.

The first is the do-it-yourself method. There are dozens of books that will show you how. But I have discovered that very few people are prepared to do it on their own. Out of the hundreds of people whom I have counseled, fewer than 2 percent buy real estate on their own. Yet about 80 percent of my clients do invest in real estate. Let us see why they choose one way over the other.

To make real-estate investments by yourself takes four things:

First, it takes *time*—lots of time. You must be willing to give up a significant portion of your otherwise spare time. That will mean, sometimes, giving up a golf or raquetball game or interrupting an otherwise quiet evening at home. Other times it will mean lost sleep because of some emergency in the middle of the night.

Second, managing real estate takes the *right kind of temperament.* You must know how to deal with tenants. Would you be too rough or too soft? If a young family with a new baby couldn't pay their rent, would you really make them move?

Third, operating real estate takes *special talents*. You need skills in negotiating with banks, with savings and loan companies, with buyers, with sellers, with tenants. You also need to be a good fix-it person. Can you fix a leaky faucet or a leaky toilet? Do you enjoy painting?

The *fourth* need is *money*. If you do not have money, you need some such equivalent as excellent credit or a benefactor. The amount of money you need depends on the price of the property and the available financing. Likely the investment will demand several thousand dollars. If you have all the above, then you should buy one of those books and try it yourself. There is little doubt that if you can perform properly you can make a lot of money.

Assuming you decide not to do it yourself, how do you invest in real estate like the 80 percent of my clients I mentioned? You do it by pooling your money with other people and investing in a real-estate limited partnership. The time, temperament, and talent are supplied by the general partner, the manager of the partnership. The most valuable partnership for you should be selected with the aid of your financial planner. You must be very selective. One of the keys to a good partnership is the past record of the general partner. The good ones have an excellent reputation that even their competitors will verify. Most public partnerships are diversified with apartment complexes, office buildings, shopping centers, and industrial complexes. In addition, many of the partnerships have properties in several different locations so they are geographically diversified. The minimum investment is from $3,000 to $5,000. Once you invest the required minimum, you can usually add money in $500 or $1,000 increments as long as the partnership remains open.

THE REAL ESTATE INVESTMENT TRUST (REIT)

The REIT is another popular form of real-estate investment. Your ownership is called a "share of beneficial interest." The minimum investment is $500 or $600. After that you can invest as little as $10 at a time. There are three types of real-estate investment trusts: equity, mortgage, and hybrid. *Equity* REITs own the real estate. *Mortgage* REITs are in the lending business; they supply financing for real-estate projects. The *hybrid* REITs are a mix of the first two.

The real-estate investment trust has been called a mutual fund specializing in real estate. That description is not entirely correct, although there are some similarities. Most REIT shares are traded in the over-the-counter market; consequently, they are considered liquid. Liquidity of this degree is unusual in a real-estate investment. But *be very cautious toward anyone who tries to get you to invest in a REIT on the basis of its liquidity.* Many REITs are priced below their original price per share. I think the claimed liquidity is an unreliable reason to invest.

When investing in an equity REIT (I think they are the most reliable because of the underlying value of the property), do so for the long term. The REIT is designed as a long-term investment for income plus tax benefits. A portion of the income is not taxed because of the depreciation that is passed on through to the investors. Most equity REITs have a fluctuating income ranging from 5 to 12 percent.

SUMMARY OF REAL-ESTATE INVESTMENT CONSIDERATIONS

Here is a brief summary of the benefits you should be aware of when investing in real estate.

Income. Depending on the purpose of the investment, income may vary from zero to 10 percent. I do not recommend most negative cash flows.

Depreciation. The paradox of real estate is that while it may be going up in price from a market-value standpoint it can at the same time be going down from an accounting standpoint. Depreciation is what will shelter the income and provide tax writeoff, reducing your taxable income.

Equity buildup. When you make a mortgage payment on a house, part of it is interest and part of it pays on the principal. While the interest is an important tax deduction, the amount of principal being paid builds equity in your house. It is like a savings account. This can amount to 2 or 3 percent a year on large income-producing properties.

Appreciation. Appreciation means the amount by which the property is going up in value each year. Although the rate of appreciation is hard to establish, I use 3 percent because you must be conservative when projecting five or ten years or further into the future. I am well aware of the 20- to 30-percent yearly appreciation that has occurred in the past, but there are real-estate cycles.

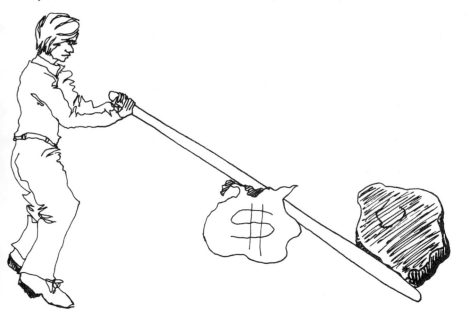

Leverage. The rate of return on your money in real estate will be increased by the last benefit, leverage.

How often have you heard that leverage is what you exercise when you use other people's money, or that leverage is money making money? The combined terms "leveraged appreciation" are often used. Here is how it works.

Let us assume that you purchased a house priced at $40,000 and you make a $10,000 down payment. That means you put 25 percent down and are carrying a mortgage of 75 percent, that is $30,000. Let us further assume that you are able to rent that house for an amount that would cover all the carrying costs (mortgage payments, insurance, taxes, and maintenance costs) and that you have no vacancies. An appreciation rate of 3 percent figures as follows for the $40,000:

$$\begin{array}{r} \$40,000 \\ \times \quad .03 \\ \hline \$\ 1,200 \end{array}$$

That means the overall value of the rental house is going up by $1,200 a year. But wait a minute! You didn't put up $40,000. What percent return is $1,200 on your $10,000 investment? *It is 12 percent.* So while the house is going up in value at only 3 percent a year and while the tenant is paying all the costs, you are making a 12-percent return on your $10,000 investment.

Summary of Annual Benefits of a Real-Estate Investment
(Assuming an Investment of $10,000)

Benefit	Percent	Dollars
Income	0–10	0–$1,000
Depreciation	(provides tax writeoff and tax-sheltered income)	
Equity buildup (reduction of principal)	2–4	$200–400
Appreciation	3	$300
Leveraged appreciation	12–25	$1,200–2,500
Totals	14–39	$1,400–3,900

This summary presents only a range of returns. In practice, some are higher; not many are lower.

Examine the Summary of Annual Benefits (page 128). If all five benefits are added, the investment summarized would have a total return on a very conservative basis of 14 to 15 percent plus the tax writeoff and any income. For obvious reasons, a real estate investment in some form warrants your consideration.

LEASING

Many users find it advantageous to lease equipment rather than own it. With owned equipment the user ties up a large amount of capital and must then depreciate it over a number of years to get the tax writeoff. With leased equipment the user does not tie up capital and simply writes off the lease payment as expense every year. Moreover, a user whose operations are sensitive to technological obsolescence may need the flexibility that can be arranged in a relatively short-term lease of long-lived equipment.

There are two approaches to investing in equipment for leasing to users. The first is to create a significant tax writeoff of 90 to 100 percent for the investor the first year, using tax breaks like *bonus depreciation, investment tax credit,* and *accelerated depreciation.* This approach applies generally to long-term leases. The primary emphasis is tax savings with possible income later. *You should be in a high tax bracket to get into this type of partnership.*

The second type of leasing partnership stresses safety with income. The income generally starts around 10 percent and may return all of your original investment within five or six years, while continuing to produce a return for several more years.

One of the most crucial items that the management of the partnership must measure is the financial stability of the lessee. The stronger the lessee is, the less the risk of a default on payments. Combine that financial strength with a three- to four-year lease period that will totally pay the equipment's cost and there is a very low risk, since the equipment will most likely continue to be leased for a period of time after the partnership has paid it off.

This kind of investment provides good income with an inflation hedge. Some partnerships have also served as recession hedges because a lot of companies will look for good used equipment during hard times. You can get into this kind of partnership for about $3,000.

Chapter 16 **Other Types of Investments**

THE STOCK MARKET

Very few laymen or experts understand the stock market. I am continually mystified by it. I do not feel that the market has a reliable degree of predictability. One of my clients once told me that because of the stock market he slept like a baby—he woke up every two hours and cried.

The stock market did not serve the average layman as a hedge against inflation or recession during the 1970s. During the recession of 1974-1975, stock prices hit record lows not seen since the crash of 1929. At the same time, inflation was in the double-digit range.

Theoretically, many stocks should be going up and worth more than their actual market price. In these individual instances, there is a strong case for saying that such a particular stock is under-valued. That means that the assets of the company may even be worth more than the market value of its stock. So why aren't the stocks selling for more? A lot of people have answers to that question, but they usually do not agree.

There is a strong correlation between current events and stock-market reactions. Innumerable things like interest rates, the dollar rising or falling overseas, peace conferences, rates of inflation, and the like affect the market and therein lies the paradox. A company may have excellent earnings and be growing at a healthy pace, yet the stock of the company may be going down or, at best, staying even.

Frustrating? Yes. Because we want to invest in American industry with a high degree of confidence. There are people who have made money in the market in recent years. Their basic strategy is to be in the market when it goes up and out when it goes down. For instance, if you were out of the market during the last recession and got back in when it started back up, you would have made substantial gains. The key is timing. Successful investors generally have excellent advice based on a proven system of timing their entries into and their exits out of the stock market. To be in the market successfully, you must have a better strategy than to buy and hold. For most people the next alternative is worth considering.

INVESTMENT FUNDS

There has been a remarkable transformation in the mutual-funds industry since 1974. The basic concept of having profes-sional managers acquire and hold and sell assets is a sound one. I did not recommend mutual funds until 1974, when the money-market funds started to come on strong. It became a good invest-ment to obtain their relatively safe high returns at the then prevailing interest rates. This also proved true in 1979 and 1980, when you could invest $2,000 to $3,000 and receive the high returns normally given only to those who could deposit $100,000 or more. *Yet you had 100-percent liquidity* any time you wanted it. You could even use the fund as a checking account, so long as the checks were over $500. Investment on these terms gives you excellent flexibility. This kind of fund is also a good vehicle to use for accumulating money for longer-term investments.

Many investment companies have created families of funds. The typical group consists of an *aggressive growth fund,* a *balanced income fund,* a *corporate bond fund,* a *municipal-bond fund,* a *money-market fund,* an *option fund,* and perhaps others. The ability to switch funds within the family becomes a key strategy in your fight against inflation. For instance, a switch could be made from a money-market fund to a growth fund. The charge for shifting is usually only $5. So, if you think the market is going up, you switch into a growth fund and go on the offensive. If the market starts down, you switch to a money fund and call on the defensive team. Essentially, you are pulling out of the market. You can purchase *timing strategies* to help you make the tactical decisions.

Some managers have become very adept at timing within the fund itself and have established very creditable records.

A small minority of investment companies have been around for a long time and have very respectable records. Because I am a registered securities principal and my license is subject to the jurisdiction of the National Association of Securities Dealers, I am restricted from listing those companies here unless I give you a prospectus. This rule is fortunate, because the funds might not be suitable for your situation. A determination of this type is made only after studying a prospectus and discussing it with your financial planner.

The day of the gun-slinging high-pressure selling of mutual funds is over. The point to remember is that the funds are alive and well and that there may be one suitable for you.

SECOND MORTGAGES

In some states second mortgages are called second "deeds of trusts." A first mortgage is the primary loan against a property.

Generally, you get a first mortgage from a bank, a savings-and-loan institution, a mortgage company, or an insurance company.

Let's assume that you own a house worth $80,000 with a first mortgage of $20,000. You thereby have $60,000 of equity in that property—cash value. Let us further assume that you want to obtain and use part of the cash value of your home. One of the ways you can do this is by finding a company or individual who lends money on a second mortgage.

If you want $20,000, the lending agent (an individual or a company) would loan you the money and you would use your house equity as collateral in the form of a second mortgage.

Lending money for second mortgages can be a good fixed-income investment. It is not an equity investment because you are loaning money at a fixed rate until a stipulated date with a prepayment penalty. Because of the prepayment penalty, many second mortgages yield more than the agreed rate of interest. Because houses are often sold before they mature, it is not unusual for a second mortgage to be paid off early. For instance, if the interest is 10 percent and there is a 2-percent prepayment penalty, you will make 12 percent on the amount prematurely paid off.

Sometimes, because of a need for cash, second mortgages are sold at a discount. That practice creates the opportunity to increase the size of the return. For instance, if there is a second mortgage worth $10,000 paying 10 percent for five years and you buy it for $8,000, then your interest has increased to 15 percent a year. Moreover, you will get a capital gain of $2,000 on your invested principal.

The best way to lend money for second mortgages is to work through an experienced company or individual specializing in the field. Examine his or its past records closely to determine what guidelines are used in deciding whether this specialist will take a second mortgage. The market value of the property and the ability of the people to pay are the two most important criteria. To make your loan safe, there should be at least a 30-percent equity left in the house (after the second mortgage) and the combined first and second mortgage payments should not take more than about 30 percent of the cash flow of the people borrowing the money.

There is no tax advantage to second mortgages; all the interest is taxable when received. Second mortgages could help hedge for inflation, they may be valuable during recessions, and generally they are not liquid.

TAX-FREE MUNICIPAL BONDS

Tax-free municipal bonds are issued by communities that have tax-exempt status on the interest paid to the buyer. Most states grant the same privilege to municipal bonds issued in their state. If you buy these bonds and they are issued in your state, you do not pay federal or state income tax on the interest.

The interest paid on these bonds is relatively low because of their favored tax status. The tax-free status acts as a government subsidy to encourage and assist municipalities in building projects. The interest paid ranges from 5 percent to 8 percent, depending on the interest-rate level at the time of issue.

These bonds should be used only by people in a high enough tax bracket to benefit from the after-tax return. For example, if you are in a 50-percent tax bracket and the yield is 6 percent, it is the equivalent of a 12-percent yield that is taxable.

Since these bonds are for a relatively long term, you should be reasonably sure you will remain in a high tax bracket for several years or you will lose the benefit.

Also, keep in mind that while the bonds may be liquid in the sense that you can sell them, there could be a question as to whether you would make a profit. Ignoring the slight risk of default, you simply compare the interest rates you receive and the overall interest-rate market. For instance, if you have bonds yielding 5 percent and the current market yield is 6 percent, you would liquidate at a loss. If the situation were reversed, you could liquidate at a profit or at least come out even. I do not consider these bonds an inflation hedge and only a possible, but questionable recession hedge with uncertain liquidity. They are strictly for someone in a 40-percent or higher tax bracket.

There are three ways to invest in tax-free bonds: either buy individual bonds or buy shares in a mutual fund or trust. Check with your financial planner.

SINGLE-PREMIUM TAX-DEFERRED ANNUITIES

Annuities in numerous forms have been around for three centuries. We are going to examine the annuity contract under which you pay a single premium (or deposit) and receive payments at some future date; in the interval, the premium/deposit earns interest, on which taxes are deferred until the earned interest is paid out to you (or to someone you designate). This *single-premium tax-deferred annuity* (SPTDA) is offered by life-insurance companies. Their strong financial positions may give the investment a high degree of safety.

The essential feature of these annuities is that the interest earned in them is *tax-deferred.* You do not have to pay taxes currently on the accumulating interest. In some cases you can defer the tax until you are 80 years old. Here is an example of the difference that the tax-deferment feature can make.

Example: If you are in the 30-percent tax bracket, a return of 7 percent before taxes is equivalent to a return of 4.9 percent after taxes. If you were to deposit $1,000 into an account paying 4.9 percent, tax free and compounded annually, it would accumulate to $1,613.45 in ten years. If you were to deposit $1,000 at 7 percent, tax deferred and compounded annually, you would end up in ten years with $1,967.15

Investment of $1,000—Ten years

Amount accumulated at 7 percent compounded annually —subject to deferred income tax	$1,967.15
Amount accumulated at 7 percent compounded annually— after income taxes paid at 30 percent (equivalent to 4.9 percent after taxes)	1,613.45
Difference	$ 353.70

So for every $1,000 you would make $353.70 more. If that were $10,000, you would have $3,537 more in ten years. The higher your tax bracket, the more you keep. The benefit of deferred taxes is the opportunity to pay the tax after your peak earning years when you are likely to be in a lower tax bracket.

There are two kinds of interest rates paid on SPTDAs—a *current* rate and a *guaranteed minimum* rate. The guaranteed minimum ranges from 3.5 to 6 percent, depending upon the company. Typically, these minimum rates are guaranteed for at least ten years and sometimes for life. The current rate is guaranteed for a much shorter period and is geared to be competitive with the current money market. Current rates can vary; as this is written they range from about 7.5 percent to 10 percent for a specified time.

There are *load* and *no-load* annuities. That is to say, some companies take expenses out of your deposit (their load) and some do not (they take no load). The load can range from 3 to 8 percent.

Companies that charge a load usually give you the right to take your money out at any time without penalty; in a sense you have already paid one.

The no-load annuities take nothing out at the time of deposit (up front), but they have a "back-end" load structure applying to surrenders and large partial withdrawals. The surrender charges may apply in time frames of anywhere from five years to lifetime. The charge may be a level percentage for a fixed number of years. However, the most common approach is to grade the charge from as high as 10 percent, going down to little or no charge after ten years. For example, the charge may mean that, if you withdraw over 7 percent (some companies permit 10 percent) of your capital in one year, you will have to pay a surrender charge for the amount withdrawn over the allowable amount. Here is one company's schedule:

Year	Surrender Charge, Percent	Year	Surrender Charge, Percent
1	7	5	3
2	6	6	2
3	5	7	1
4	4	8	0

Just about every company guarantees that you get your principal back, even if you pull out in the first year.

The annuities are liquid. You can cash them in at any time you want.

The proceeds of an annuity do not go through probate on the death of the annuitant if they are paid to a named beneficiary.

The first-in-first-out (FIFO) method of accounting allows you to consider your withdrawals as a return of capital. Since that capital withdrawal does not include the interest, you can take a withdrawal on which you will pay no taxes. Once your principal is consumed, you will be subject to taxation on your withdrawals.

Your removal of funds should be irregular—different amounts at different times—so the Internal Revenue Service won't take the position that you have actually annuitized your contract and force you to forfeit the tax benefit.

There are two methods of withdrawal. One is informal; you simply take occasional withdrawals. The other method is to annuitize the contract. The latter method means that you direct the annuity company to keep your money in return for a guaranteed amount of money, paid monthly, for anywhere from three years to life. This aspect of the annuity needs to be managed on the basis of your financial situation.

No-Load Single-Premium Tax-Deferred Annuity— The Concept

Phase I— Accumulation Period	Phase II— Income Period (Two Ways)
1. Safe	1. Withdrawal prior to age limit
2. Liquid	2. Annuitization
3. No current taxes on interest	a. Lifetime income
4. Competitive interest (two rates)	b. Principal is protected
5. Interest guaranteed for specified	from creditors
times	c. Several options from
6. 100 percent of principal earns	which to choose
interest	
7. 100-percent money-back guarantee	
8. No probate with named beneficiary	
9. FIFO accounting of irregular	
withdrawals	

Look carefully at the example comparing a regular savings account with the tax-deferred annuity account. Assuming a 7-percent rate of return on both, it shows the regular savings account taxed all the way through. No taxation is reflected on the annuity side during the 24-year period. The comparison shows that there is $206,000 more in the annuity at the beginning of year 25. The difference at this point is that the $141,000 left in the savings account will not be taxed; tax has already been paid on it. All but $2,000 of the $347,000 left in the annuity is subject to income tax. Even so, through proper management of withdrawals (and with careful guidance by your financial planner), the annuity will come out substantially ahead. This example is used only to illustrate the differences. In fact, you should not make consistent withdrawals to avoid disqualifying the tax benefit. If you chose to actually annuitize, the interest part of your monthly payment would be taxable and the part that is a partial return of your principal would not be taxable.

You can purchase single-premium tax-deferred annuities for a minimum of $2,500 and you should plan to use them for at least six years. This kind of annuity is not a very good inflation fighter, but it is a good recession hedge, low in risk and liquid, and it has a tax-deferral benefit.

Example: Regular Savings Account Compared with Tax-Deferred Annuity Account

Assumptions:
    Single deposit or single premium, $100,000
    Accumulation period, 10 years with no withdrawals
    Tax bracket during accumulation period, 50 percent
    Tax bracket during withdrawal period, 30 percent
    Interest, 7 percent compounded annually.

	Regular Savings	Tax-Deferred Annuity
Accumulation period (10 years):		
Amount deposited	$100,000	$100,000
Amount after 10 years' accumulation	141,000 (after tax)	196,000
Withdrawal period (14 years):		
Amount withdrawn each year	$ 6,911 (see Note A)	$ 7,000 (see Note B)
Total of withdrawals	$ 96,754	$ 98,000
Balance after withdrawals	$141,000	$347.000
More in the annuity		$206,000

Note A: The accumulated amount of $141,000 earns interest at 7 percent annually, which is $9,870. After being taxed in the 30-percent income-tax bracket, this leaves $6,911 of spendable income per year, or $96,754 for the fourteen-year period. It should be noted that the $141,000 is "after taxes"—that is, no additional taxes will have to be paid.

Note B: The accumulated amount of $196,000 earns interest at 7 percent during the first year (or $13,270) and after $7,000 is withdrawn the remaining interest continues to accumulate. The continuing accumulation over the fourteen-year withdrawal period brings the balance up to $347,000. It is important to note that tax will have to be paid on the $347,000 as you withdraw it or as payments are received if you amortize it. You would have to continually exceed a 60-percent tax bracket to end up with less than the $141,000 in the savings account.

A SAVINGS ANNUITY

If you prefer to leave some money in a savings account at a bank or at a savings and loan, consider using an annuity that you can build with additional deposits in your savings account.

In practice this kind of annuity will allow you to have your savings accumulate on a tax-deferred basis, just like the SPTDA.

In a technical sense the savings on deposit becomes an asset of the annuity operator, usually an insurance company, classified as admitted assets. A small percent of the earnings is taken out as a charge by the insurance company. The first year the fee is higher than that from the second year on. Because you do not have to pay taxes currently on the interest, you will end up with substantially more money growing in your acccount. Only four or five insurance companies currently have this product. Your savings institution must have an agreement with the insurance company to provide it. Before taking your funds out of your savings or bank account, ask the management if they plan on making this annuity plan available to all depositors. If they do not, then consider transferring your funds to an institution that will be able to provide you with the benefit. Doing so is well worth your attention.

Since the laws on this kind of annuity seem likely to change, always obtain current information before taking action.

Chapter 17 **Tangibles**

DIAMONDS

Diamonds are rare and are perhaps the world's most coveted gems. Since 1939 investment-grade diamonds have not been devalued once. They can be an excellent investment, but you should keep their purchase in balance with other investments in your financial spectrum.

Be careful. The fervor of the late 1970s has led some people to be caught by deceivers. Some people, unbelievably, purchased diamonds under high-pressure phone calls or face-to-face hard-sell techniques. *No investment in existence warrants that approach or your acceptance of it.*

Diamonds are graded in almost 2,000 categories of quality. While it is true that all diamonds are appreciating, the very best diamonds appreciate much faster. Your decision to purchase diamonds as an investment requires at least the following three considerations:

First, buy only the very best diamonds. You can determine the best by being specific in your diamond selection. Don't just walk into a jewelry store and ask for "a good-looking half-carat diamond." Investigate the four C's.

Carat weight. For investment purposes, try to keep under 2 carats; diamonds that weigh ½ to 1 carat are preferable. That range is the most liquid.

Cut. Purchase stones that are well cut in the round brilliant style and always demand near ideal proportions—not too deep and not too shallow.

Clarity. As a minimum, look for only very slightly (VS) impaired or preferably very very slightly (VVS) impaired stones, allowing only the fewest microscopic imperfections.

Color. Buy at least H in color to assure a good-quality white stone.

These are the four categories used in grading your stones. Obtain at least one certified gemologist's appraisal on the stone. Better, obtain independent appraisals from two. Each diamond is like a thumbprint; no two are alike.

Second, purchase an investment diamond at wholesale not retail value. There are even different wholesale values, depending on markups for handling costs and convenience.

Third, investigate the company or source from which you purchase a diamond. The company should be highly reputable and a direct importer of top-quality diamonds. The best companies buy from the major cutting factories, who participate in the DeBeers purchase program.

DeBeers is the international cartel that controls 80 percent of the world market in diamonds. It is located in London. Its market control is complete. Only highly respected diamond-cutting companies are invited to participate in the diamond "sights" or sales held about ten times a year by DeBeers. DeBeers sets the price, determines the quality, and sets the quantity it will sell to any company. No question on the diamond's price, quality, or quantity is tolerated. Disagreements result in the companies' being expelled from the prestigious sights.

Here is an example of the increase in the value of diamonds since 1974. A ½-carat VVS H stone has appreciated from $419 to $2,000 in 1978. A 1-carat stone went from about $1,855 to $8,400. Astounding increases! No one knows whether the history of the last few years will repeat itself. The main point is that diamonds, properly purchased, will probably continue to go up in value. Diamonds can serve both as an inflation hedge and a recession hedge, are easily transportable, and offer a fair degree of liquidity. On the other hand, they give you no cash flow and there is no tax advantage.

GOLD AND SILVER

Gold and silver were once rigorously linked to this country's money supply. Up until 1934 a $10 (or larger) bill might carry this

imprint: "This certifies that there has been deposited in the Treasury of the United States of America ten dollars (or other amount) in gold coin payable to the bearer on demand." This bill was legal tender—if you owed someone $10 and offered this bill to him, he had to take it. Other United States currency—paper money—carried similar references to metal money. On silver certificates it read: "This certifies that there is on deposit in the Treasury of the United States of America ten dollars (or other amount) in silver payable to the bearer on demand." Silver certificates are no longer issued, and gold certificates since 1934 have been issued only to Federal Reserve banks. If you should chance to find an old silver or gold certificate—a bill of $10 or any other denomination—my advice is not to take it to the Treasury and try to get gold or silver unless you have a sense of humor. Now our paper money says, "This note is legal tender for all debts, public and private." And on the other side it says, "In God We Trust."

Our money now fluctuates according to a floating international supply-and-demand situation. There are several books written on the subject of silver and gold in relation to our money. Here I want to highlight one main theme—the importance of a viable medium of exchange: a money.

There are four prerequisites for a lasting medium of exchange: (1) It must be durable. (2) It must be uniform in quality. (3) It must be limited in supply. (4) It must have uses that are uniquely found in it alone.

Money no longer meets these requirements. Silver and gold do. That is why the price of both goes up significantly during times of economic insecurity. Industrial, psychological, political, supply-and-demand, and many other factors cause people to find precious metals a safe haven in troubled times.

Some of my most conservative clients, who during good times have tended to laugh at the gold fever, have been some of the first to call me during troubled times and ask if they shouldn't hedge a bit with some silver or gold.

There is no way I can predict what is going to happen to the United States economy. The best thing is to be ready for any contingency without getting out of balance with your money. Consider buying gold and silver as a hedge, not necessarily as an investment. Owning them is like owning an insurance policy.

My suggestion is to own some silver and gold coins and hold them indefinitely. Consider the money you have put into them as a defense measure to protect yourself against bad times.

RARE COINS

Apart from the gold and silver coins that might be considered commodities, you may be considering rare-coin collecting. The strategy is basically the same as that of stamp collecting. You want to find rare coins whose demand is greater than their supply. Such coins are definitely a good area of investment to hedge for inflation and recession. Coins are sold at auctions and coin stores. Be sure to use an expert in acquiring these coins. The number of investors has increased dramatically in recent years and should continue to make rare coins a good investment.

STAMPS

Until 1970, three-quarters of the people who collected stamps did so as a hobby. The other quarter were not hobbyists—they were investors. The percent figures have now turned around. The majority of people now collecting stamps are doing so for investment purposes. The object of investing in quality stamps is to hold them and make a good profit. There are enough people in the world interested in the quality and price of rare stamps to make them viable investment material.

If you invest $5,000 in stamps, you will have 15 to 20 quality stamps. If you hold them for three years you should be well into the profit area. When you decide to sell them, expect to wait at least three to four months to obtain a good price. You could just take them to a local stamp dealer, but you would probably get less than the best price for them. The best way to sell stamps is through one of the respectable auction houses. My feeling about any collectible, such as stamps and coins, is to use them only if you already have an interest in them.

Instead of considering stamp collecting as just a hobby, acknowledge it as a serious investment and proceed in a scientific and businesslike manner.

OTHER COLLECTIBLES—ART WORKS AND ANTIQUES

Art works and antiques can make excellent investments. Considerable research and knowledge is necessary to invest in the right objects. If you already have interest in these areas you could make them a serious investment area.

SUMMARY

There is a whole galaxy of investments. I have mentioned only a few that have served many people well over the years. Experience has taught me that it is best to stay fairly mainstream and cautious when putting your serious money to work. The decisions are like the lesson we learn from the tale of the tortoise and the hare. Persistence and consistency will almost invariably lead you to your goal. Continually analyze and evaluate your progress in the light of your goals. Use the investment chart to make sure you do not get out of balance.

Chapter 18 **Restructuring Your Hayden Investment Chart**

In Chapter 5, we looked at a couple who had $40,000 positioned in three different places. Their objectives were as follows:

1. Low to medium risk
2. To have their money consistently grow faster than inflation
3. To have about 50 percent of their funds in a low-risk position
4. To have 30 percent of their funds hedged against recession
5. To have 60 percent of their funds hedged against inflation
6. If possible to have no management responsibilities

They chose to reposition their money in a money-market fund, a single-premium tax deferred annuity, a real-estate partnership, and a cable-television partnership.

Following the steps outlined in Chapter 5, let us look at their chart on page 148. The answer in each area—yes or no—is their answer after a thorough discussion of all the investments. They decided to sell their rental unit and to liquidate all their stock. The money was then repositioned as is shown. As you can see, these people have significantly increased their advantage in almost every area. Over 87 percent of the $40,000 is creating some form of tax advantage. Since they were concerned about inflation, they were able to have 62.5 percent of their funds hedged for this contingency. This was done while still increasing their recession hedge.

The clients also wanted 25 percent of their funds to remain liquid, and they were able to keep that portion in line with their objective. They disengaged their high-risk investments and shifted most of their funds to medium risk, while retaining a low-risk ratio of 37.5 percent.

For the summary comparing their investments before and after planning, see the chart on page 149.

This is a process you can start on your own. With a little practice you will begin to see where you would reposition your money to get closer to your objectives. You may wish to consider using a financial planner to assist you. Each time you have a little more money, or want to measure yourself, go back to your chart and see where you are. This financial experience can be most rewarding.

The Hayden Investment Chart— $40,000 Repositioned

	Investments				
	Money Market Fund	Single-Premium Tax-Deferred Annuity	Real-Estate Limited Partner-ship	Cable-Television Limited Partner-ship	*Totals*
Amount	$5,000	$10,000	$15,000	$10,000	$40,000
Percent of total	12.50	25	37.50	25	100

Criterion					*Percent Meeting Criterion*
Risk { Medium			37.50%	25%	62.50
{ Low	12.50%	25%			37.50
Tax advantage	No	Yes	Yes	Yes	87.50
Inflation hedge	No	No	Yes	Yes	62.50
Recession hedge	Yes	Yes	No	Yes	62.50
Freedom from management	Yes	Yes	Yes	Yes	100.00
Liquidity	Yes	Yes	No	No	37.50

IMPLEMENTING THE PLAN

Once you realize how you can improve your situation, do not hesitate to put your new plan of action to work. Procrastination is one of the main reasons people do not reach their goals. You probably already decided to implement your plan. Now is the time to act.

Analyzing Progress Toward Goals

	Before Repositioning, Percent	After Repositioning, Percent	Percent Change
Risk { Low	37.50	37.50	None
Medium	37.50	62.50	+25
High	25	0	−25
Tax advantage	37.50	87.50	+50
Inflation hedge	37.50	62.50	+25
Recession hedge	37.50	62.50	+25
Freedom from management	37.50	100.00	+62.50
Liquidity	62.50	37.50	−25*

* Consistent with goals.

Result: The clients' money is now positioned in a way that is more consistent with their goals.

Chapter 19 **Estate-Planning Comments**

A farmer and his wife were amazed to discover that they were worth over $3 million! Until we evaluated their farm property with them, they had thought they were thousandaires but not millionaires. They were millionaires—about $3 million. Their attorneys, for some unknown reason, had not even advised them to draw up wills. Had the husband died, the estate and inheritance taxes would have been almost $1.5 million. With little or no appreciable liquidity in the estate, the properties would have been auctioned off at distress prices just to pay these taxes. Fortunately, now, that will not happen, because in the process of discussing estate planning with them we were able to zero in on this major problem area. I called in an attorney who is an estate-planning specialist. He drew the necessary legal documents and we jointly were able to develop strategies that will save the farmer and his wife more than a million dollars!

Not all situations are that dramatic, but over the past decade I can easily count up to more than $100 million that I have been able to keep in estates rather than have it go to federal and state governments in taxes as a result of little or no estate planning.

There are at least two reasons why you should plan your estate now. First, the time of any death is already one of great trauma for the survivors. That is not the time for them to try to figure out estate problems. Second, the unplanned estate may end up paying far too much in probate costs, federal estate taxes, and state inheritance taxes.

Governments make us pay for passing our estates on to our

children. I have not, however, noticed any government trying to help us build our estates. Quite to the contrary, they try very hard, through sometimes exorbitant taxation, to keep us from accumulating any wealth. And if we nevertheless succeed, then when we die the tax collectors try to take it away from our heirs. They literally get us coming and going.

No financial plan is complete until you have provided for the ultimate disposition of your estate. This is a legal matter and calls for an attorney who is a specialist in estate planning. You may already have an attorney, but if your estate is worth over $250,000 you should probably have a specialist to advise you and to draw up the legal documents. (And with today's inflation, more and more people are finding themselves about the $250,000 mark.) Through the right kind of arrangement, you could save such an estate as much as $25,000. Remember that the estate may include life insurance.

There has been a lot written about avoiding probate. In the light of recent laws it may or may not be significantly advantageous to avoid probate; again there are no pat answers. The best course depends on the size of your estate. Under no circumstances should you draw up your own legal documents. Federal and state laws are far too complex for you to undertake estate disposition as a do-it-yourself project. I am not trying to pour your money into the coffers of the legal profession; however, some dollars spent now can save your beneficiaries many dollars and a lot of headaches after you pass on.

The role of your planner is to pinpoint problem areas in the preparations for the distribution of your estate. The planner will help you with all the questions you wondered about, but were afraid to ask. Most importantly, the financial planner will act as coordinator with a good estate-planning attorney to help solve your problems.

There are three primary goals to keep in mind when planning your estate. They are:

1. That your estate goes to whom you want to receive it
2. That it goes to the recipient when and in the manner that you wish
3. That it goes to your beneficiaries with the lowest possible cost consistent with your objectives

BE PRACTICAL

Some married couples want the surviving spouse to receive the maximum possible, and also their children when the surviving spouse dies. Other couples are not primarily concerned about their children receiving the entire estate, particularly if making the arrangement is going to increase legal costs out of proportion to the amount of inheritance involved.

It is not within the scope of this book to cover all the details of estate planning. If you want more information about this subject, buy a book written by an author who is knowledgeable about your specific state. There are significant differences in state laws and inheritance taxes.

Just about everyone should have a will. With a will, you can specify who will handle your estate and who will receive it. If you have no will, then a judge will appoint an administrator and the settlement of the estate could prove costly to everyone involved.

A *living trust* may achieve the objective of a will, although many attorneys are against the idea. If your estate is $250,000 or more, it is something you should consider. A living trust is established by a legal document that a husband and wife sign. Most of their assets are put into the trust. If they are the trustees, they have complete control over these assets; and they should be the trustees, barring unique circumstances. At death, the assets in trust avoid probate and delay, their affairs are kept private, and costs are saved.

Other trusts can be formed to create substantial tax savings. I must emphasize that your estate-planning team must include, as a primary member, a good-estate planning attorney.

PART FIVE **FINANCIAL PLANNING AND THE FINANCIAL PLANNER**

Chapter 20 **Finding Reliable Advice — How to Evaluate Your Sources**

Financial planning is building and insulating assets and assuring a sound financial present and future while meeting your goals.

Financial planning is a process that includes:

1. Defining goals and objectives
2. Relating these goals and objectives to your resources of time, assets, income, cash flow, and liabilities
3. Implementing strategies, including the possible repositioning of assets and redirecting of cash flow to reach your objectives
4. The use of technical and social sciences to achieve that result

A financial planner must be an objective diagnostician and a problem solver. He is a conductor, orchestrating the various elements within your financial symphony. Just as a conductor need not know how to play the bassoon, the oboe, and the flute, so a planner need not possess all the varied skills of an attorney, an accountant, a life-insurance representative, and an expert in the other related fields that have a direct effect on your finances. But as the conductor has a good overview and general knowledge of all the instruments in his charge, so must the planner have a view over all the elements of the financial spectrum.

Henry Ford was not a well-educated man. When asked the secret of his success, his answer was, "I don't have to know everything. I have a row of buttons on my desk, and each button calls an expert in a different area. All I have to know is *which* button to push." A financial planner has to know which buttons or series of buttons to push, and not to be afraid to push them.

In selecting a financial planner, you should look for someone with a basic background knowledge of taxes, investments, savings, insurance, retirement planning, estate planning, business management, and economics. There are no universally accepted or widely published standards to help you select a planner. At the present time, just about anyone can pick up the title of "financial planner" and run with it.

For example, there are people who call themselves financial planners yet work in only one area, sell some one product, such as real estate or stocks or mutual funds or insurance, and know almost nothing beyond that specialty. They may be very good in their particular area (whichever *one* it is) but they will lack the overall knowledge of the multifaceted field of financial planning and consequently will be woefully short of the necessary experience that brings about objectivity. Stay away from any "planner" who shows a strong feeling or bias toward only one resource in the financial variety.

It is my belief that only a few who represent themselves as financial planners are actually qualified to perform the function. The rest are what I call "product peddlers." They use the title "financial planner" to help market their products with little if any thought as to the overall needs of their clients. Some of the people calling themselves financial planners do so without the knowledge, training, or experience to represent themselves as such. Then there are others who *know* they *don't know* what they are doing but proceed nonetheless, with only their own greedy needs in mind. Be careful. In the next few pages I will give you some guidelines for choosing a planner.

The current state of financial planning has much in common with the field of medicine a hundred years ago. Then there were negligible requirements to be licensed as a physician, or no

requirements at all. Some physicians served a short apprentice-
ship and then set up practice. Those were the days when one of the
treatments for a fever was attaching leeches to the patient's body
to suck and drain away "excess blood." Medicine was primitive;
not until the field was approached scientifically and appropriate
ethical standards were adopted did the profession begin to make
progress and the patients start living longer. Currently, a lot of
financial leeching is going on in this country. But regardless of the
chicanery on the part of some in the field, the country also has a
healthy professional financial-planning movement growing
rapidly. The International Association of Financial planners is
working diligently to maintain ethical professional standards
aimed at clearing away the confusion that surrounds the profession.

PLANNER SELECTION

You need not be a financial planner to select a good one. You just
need to know the right questions to ask; the person you are
appraising should have the right answers. If he or she doesn't have
them, try another one. Here are some questions.

1. *How long have you been practicing financial planning, and
how were you trained?* A person who has been a seasoned estate
planner in the insurance field or a stock broker, trust officer,
accountant, or attorney, and who has additional study and
experience in related fields has a good balanced background to be a
planner. The planner should be open-minded about helping you
reach *your* financial goals. He or she should encourage you to
participate in the planning. The person who does more talking
than listening may not have your best interest at heart. It is not
only the length but also the quality of training that is important.
2. *How are financial planners compensated?* There are five
ways a planner may be paid: (a) by a fee set or agreed; (b) by a
commission from those whose various products are sold when
your plan is implemented; (c) by a combination fee *and* commission; (d) by a fee *or* a commission at the option of the client; (e) by a
charge computed as a percent of assets. A fee is usually similar to
that charged by an attorney or an accountant and should be
approved by you, in the form of an estimate, before the planning

proceeds. The planner should always disclose to you how he or she makes money.

3. *What licenses do you hold?* If a planner holds only one license and is dependent for his income on the commissions paid from the sale of one or two products, he may be heavily biased in favor of the same one or two resources. Stay away from this kind of situation. Look for someone who is licensed to handle several kinds of investment vehicles and can represent all of them without putting pressure on you to purchase any one.

4. *If you handle life insurance, how many companies do you represent?* Don't deal with a single-company life-insurance salesman. If a "planner" is the captive agent of one life-insurance company, show him the door or find your way out of his.

5. *If you handle investments, who does the due diligence on the investments you represent?* If your planner handles investments, he is a registered representative or a registered principal, and perhaps also with a New York Stock Exchange firm. Every good securities firm has a department which critically evaluates investments and approves only those that meet a strict set of guidelines. This screening process is called *due diligence.* The representative himself must screen an investment to make sure that it is appropriate for the client in question. Securities being considered may have an outstanding report from the company handling them, yet not meet the goal of the investor. There are many people who put together their own group of investments and try to sell them to the public under the title of "financial planning." And while it is possible that these investments could be sound and make a fine return for the investors, the purchase of investments from people who operate in this method is very risky. Some of these people may not hold licenses of any kind, and indeed under current law they are not required to have them. They may be *principals* of their investments (see No. 7 below). The license is important, because it provides for some control and regulation of the planner. The National Association of Securities Dealers is a self-governing body that supervises its members carefully. It establishes and enforces regulations that protect the public. Let me say again, be *sure* you know who does the due diligence on the securities you might be buying. Always ask what securities company the planner represents.

6. *Do you deal with private placements?* Any licensed repre-

sentatives who handle private placements that are not approved by their securities company are violating the rules of the National Association of Securities Dealers. In the past, enough people were burned on hot deals offered this way to prompt rules that now help prevent that practice.

7.   *Are you ever a principal in any investments you recommend?* You must be aware of any potential conflicts of interest. In most cases, it is better if the planner is not involved in the investment as a principal or as a general partner. It is certainly acceptable for a planner to invest in the same investments that you do.

8.   *Is it necessary to work with my accountant and attorney?* Yes! If the planner says "no," get your hat and say good-bye.

9.   *Are you a Registered Investment Advisor?* A person who is charging a fee and is offering investment advice should be a Registered Investment Advisor (RIA) as required by the Securities and Exchange Commission. There are two ways people can be covered as Registered Investment Advisors: first, as individuals with direct registration; second, through the securities firm with which they are licensed. In either case they are required to present you with information defining their business and with some personal information about themselves.

10.   *Are you a Certified Financial Planner and a member of the International Association of Financial Planners? If so, of which chapter?* A planner can be certified and be a member of the IAFP and still not be the person you want to have handle your financial affairs. But the chance of being pleased with the work done for you is higher if the planner is active in the recognized association that oversees the conduct of its members. The IAFP is dedicated to the highest of ethical standards and provides a *forum* for the development of the best of professional practices. Its Standards of Professional Conduct and its Code of Ethics are printed in full as appendixes at the end of this book. You will be wise to read both of them in full to understand what the IAFP feels you should expect of your financial planner.

(It should be noted that the College of Financial Planning and the International Association of Financial Planners are independent organizations that maintain cordially cooperative relations. "Certified Financial Planner" is a registered trade mark of the College of Financial Planning, which is discussed below.)

11.   *Would you give me the names of three of your clients with whom I might talk to assess your professional competence?* If a

planner gives you references, do indeed call them. If he shows reluctance to give you a list of satisfied clients, you should show a *marked* reluctance to give him your business.

CRITERIA FOR PROFESSIONAL CERTIFICATION

A stiff set of requirements must be satisfied in order to earn certification as a Certified Financial Planner. *First*, a candidate must complete five courses of study and pass a very tough examination at the end of each course. The five courses are: (1) Counseling the Individual; (2) Investments, Income, and Taxation Management; (3) Risk Management and Retirement Planning; (4) Professional Management and Technical Services; (5) Counseling for the Business and Professional Person.

Second, the candidate must earn a combination of at least five credits in educational and occupational areas by the time of graduation.

Third, the candidate must present evidence of satisfactory work experience in the financial-services industry. This evidence must include written attestation of his or her capability from three clients and letters of recommendation from two business associates.

The College of Financial Planning, located in Denver, Colorado, is the institution that grants this certification.

Other institutions are moving to meet the need for professional education in financial planning. Brigham Young University in Provo, Utah, was the first university in the country to offer an academic degree in Financial Planning; its 1980 class had its first graduating majors. Starting in 1980, Golden Gate University in San Francisco became the second institution. Golden Gate now offers a Master of Science degree in Financial Planning and a Master of Business Administration specialization in Financial Planning. The New York Institute of Finance has courses for a Professional Financial Planner Development Program, developed in close collaboration with the International Institute of Financial Planners.

THE CODE OF ETHICS

The Certified Financial Planner is bound by a code of ethics that:

1. Places the interests of the client first.
2. Requires a high degree of personal integrity.
3. Encourages a professional level of conduct in association with peers and others involved in the practice of financial planning.
4. Establishes individual responsibility for knowledge of the various laws and regulations, not only in letter but also in spirit.
5. Discourages sensational, exaggerated, and unwarranted statements.
6. Encourages prudent and responsible actions.

THE STATE OF THE ART

The art and practice of financial planning are in transition. "It is the independent financial planner that leads the field at this time. The institutions, insurance companies, stock brokerage firms, banks, and savings and loans haven't figured out how to use financial planning for everybody yet. No institution is a recognized leader in the field. Very few financial institutions understand Financial Planning as a *process*. Most view it as a separate product." That was the finding of a study done by a major research institute (*Financial Planning in the 1980s*, copyright SRI International 1979). The major institutions are looking for the independent, established financial planner to help them learn how to do professional planning. It is the independent who is flexible enough to make breaks with traditional lines of thinking in order to create a service geared to the client's needs.

Consider financial planning as a *process*, not as a product: the process through which to reach your goals and learn winning strategies. As the SRI study indicated, most institutions design financial planning solely as a *product*.

The first institution that puts together a real *service* will make a valuable contribution to you—the client or prospective client—and to the entire industry. If its practioners are committed to taking you through a *process* to help you achieve your goals and if they are people-oriented, not just product-oriented, you will see a financial evolution in this country that will do a hundred times more for you than the government ever has. There is no question that our individual freedoms will be enhanced through professional financial planning.

In conclusion, I would like to share with you some of my reasons for having become a financial planner.

Years ago, before I had entered the profession, I was sitting at my desk when I received a call from a life-insurance salesman. I bought. Weeks later, a friend introduced me to an attorney who said I should have a will. Fine—I bought. At lunch one day I met a stockbroker who said I should invest in American industry. I bought. Not long after that, I met a banker at a social gathering, and he told me I should have a savings account. I bought again. I was beginning to think that I had my financial affairs in good order.

But over the years, as problems kept appearing on my financial scene, I realized that none of these "advisers" knew each other or knew what my problems might be in the areas where they were not involved. And often their advice was conflicting.

As I have gained more experience in the financial-services industry I have sensed a real need to coordinate all of these skills for clients. That is what led to my becoming a Certified Financial Planner. I have a real sense of achievement when I see the smiles on the faces of clients whose financial affairs I have been able to coordinate so they are working toward their goals. That's what financial planning is about. Hopefully, you will have this same sense of fulfillment.

Epilogue It's Your Money—
Use It or Lose It

This book has been an attempt to give you a common-sense approach that will lead to your financial success. No one book can give you all the financial details you may need. So use this book as you would use a large-scale map that gives you the main highways for travel. More detailed maps would show you the streets of the cities in which you are interested. The detailed financial maps are available through qualified financial planners.

Appendices

Some Terms Used in Financial Planning

accident insurance One kind of *disability insurance*; see *disability insurance*.

add-on minimum tax A minimum income tax levied on holders of certain tax preference items: sec Chapter 6. For detailed information, obtain Form 4625 from the Internal Revenue Service.

alternative minimum tax A minimum tax levied on holders of certain tax preference items; see Chapter 6. For detailed information, obtain Form 6251 from the Internal Revenue Service.

annual renewable term life-insurance policy A life-insurance contract that runs for one year only, at the end of which it may be renewed at a higher premium; see Chapter 10.

annuity An income purchased by the investment of principal according to agreed or stipulated conditions. See Chapter 16.

assets The items of value that a person or organization owns. They may be money, objects, or financial obligations.

automobile insurance A *casualty insurance*; see *casualty insurance*. It includes various specific protections. See Chapter 12.

capital gain The increase in the price of an investment between the purchase and the sale. The gain is *short-term* if the investment is held less than one year, *long-term* if it is held a year or more.

casualty insurance Insurance that reimburses the insured for losses to property and for certain kinds of personal liabilities. See Chapter 12.

Consumer Price Index A measure of price-level changes for a standard assortment of consumer goods and services, compiled and published by the Bureau of Labor Statistics of the United States Department of Labor.

creditor A person or firm to which money is owed by a debtor.

debtor a person or firm that owes money to a creditor.

deferred taxes On certain kinds of income, tax liability is incurred at times later than that when the income is earned and payment is thereby deferred. See Chapter 7.

deposit term insurance policy A life-insurance contract for term insurance, under which the insured pays a higher premium the first year and accumulates a cash value that matures tax-free in the tenth year. See Chapter 10.

developmental drilling An intermediate-risk venture in the oil-and-gas business, available as limited-partnership investment. See Chapter 15.

disability insurance Insurance that provides income or a lump sum in the event of the insured's being disabled. The specific protections vary widely. See Chapter 11.

diversification Variety in investments or undertakings, such as ownership of some equities, some fixed-return securities, some real estate, or some tangible objects of value. Also, in agriculture, combinations of different crops.

encumbrance A financial obligation, an ownership qualification, or a restriction on use that affects the value or liquidity of an asset.

endowment insurance policy A life-insurance contract under which the insured pays premiums that include savings in addition to pure insurance, the savings component becoming equal to the face amount after a stipulated number of years. See Chapter 10.

equity Ownership of an interest in the profits of a business operation, as distinguished from an obligation that entitles the holder to receive a fixed amount of money. Also, the portion of the value of a piece of property that exceeds the amount of obligations (such as mortgages) owed on it.

expenditures The money or assets spent or paid out by a person or a firm.

exploratory drilling A high-risk venture in the oil-and-gas business, available as limited-partnership investment. See Chapter 15.

financial statement A formal description of the financial condition of a person or firm. It includes a list of assets and liabilities, a summary of income and expenditures, and sometimes a cash-flow projection. See Chapter 4.

general partner The managing partner in a business venture that is owned by limited partners. See Chapter 15.

health insurance Insurance that reimburses the insured for stipulated health-care and medical expenses. See Chapter 11.

hedge To protect oneself against a financial hazard. Thus, to own an investment that is stable in value, not likely to decline severely in price. An investment that has the qualities described in the preceding definitions, especially an investment that will rise in value during an inflationary period or that will retain its value during a recession.

homeowner's insurance A *casualty insurance;* see *casualty insurance.*

homestead A legal status applicable to a person's dwelling house, which confers certain protections against seizure to satisfy creditors.

income The money or assets received by a person or firm.

Individual Retirement Account (IRA) A tax shelter for persons not covered by any other kind of retirement plan. See Chapter 8.

inflation The increase in price level over a period of time. It is expressed as a percent of the price level at the beginning of the period.

investment An ownership or an interest in the ownership of a business venture or a piece of real or personal property, acquired for the purpose of receiving income or realizing a profit when the investment is sold.

investment fund A business form in which investors purchase shares with money which in turn is invested via professional managers in various vehicles. Also called a *mutual fund.* See Chapter 16.

investment tax credit A credit against income-tax obligation allowed to a business operation that makes capital investments deemed beneficial to the national economy and authorized by tax laws.

Keogh Plan A retirement tax shelter for self-employment income; see Chapter 8.

leverage The advantage gained by an investor who can use money borrowed at fixed interest to control or own investments that return income or profits exceeding the interest cost. See Chapter 15.

liability Money that a person or firm owes to other persons or firms or to a government. The one that owes is called the *debtor.* The one owed is called the *creditor.*

limited partnership A business form in which the investor risks only the amount of his investment and thus becomes a limited partner, usually taking no part in management. The investments of the many limited partners are pooled and managed by a *general partner.* See Chapter 15.

liquidity The capacity to sell or buy an asset readily at full value. Money is a completely liquid asset. A piece of real estate may be not at all liquid; that is, it may not be saleable at a desired time although intrinsically valuable.

living trust A legal device designed usually to let a surviving spouse/or child take possession of a decedent's asset while avoiding probate costs and delays. See Chapter 19.

load A charge made by mutual-fund and annuity operators against investments in such vehicles. See Chapter 16.

money-market fund An investment fund that holds and trades in such money-market instruments as acceptances, commercial paper, high-interest certificates of deposit, and similar obligations. See Chapter 16.

mortgage A legal instrument under which a loan is secured by a lien on property. *First mortgages* are commonly used to finance home purchases. *Second mortgages* employ the equity in the property as security for funds to be reinvested or otherwise used. See Chapter 16.

net worth The difference between the liabilities and the assets of a person or a firm. The amount of the assets is equal to the sum of the liabilities and the net worth. In a business firm's financial statement net worth may be called *proprietorship*. If the net worth is negative, the person or firm is insolvent.

paid-up whole life insurance policy A life-insurance contract under which the insured pays premiums only until a stipulated age, typically 65. See Chapter 10.

pension plan A plan under which corporation employees or other beneficiaries continue to receive income after retirement and sometimes after other termination of employment. See Chapter 8.

profit-sharing plan A plan under which corporation employees accumulate agreed portions of the employer's profits, usually withdrawn by the employee at or after retirement or other termination of employment. Such plans vary widely. See Chapter 8.

pure life-insurance policy A life-insurance contract under which the insurer accepts the entire risk of the insured person's dying and the insured pays for the risk only, without associated savings features.

real-estate investment (REIT) A business form for dealing in real estate mortgages and/or equities. See Chapter 15.

recession A decline in business activity, often accompanied by a fall in prices and employment and by reduced availability of credit.

refinancing Borrowing money on the equity in a home or other asset, usually for investment in vehicles that offer tax advantages or income that will more than offset the additional cost of the borrowing. See Chapter 14.

repositioning Liquidating investments and investing the proceeds in other vehicles that offer improvements in income, tax advantage, consistency with objectives, or other desired features.

savings annuity An annuity contract involving a savings institution and an insurance company under which interest is accumulated on a tax-deferred basis. See Chapter 16.

Securities and Exchange Commission An independent federal commission charged with protecting investors and the public against malpractice in the markets for financial instruments, and with other duties.

single-premium tax-deferred annuity An annuity contract under which liability for income taxes is deferred until a later date more advantageous for the owner. See Chapter 16.

tangibles Things of value deemed suitable as investment vehicles because they will probably appreciate in price to compensate for inflation or exceed it. See Chapter 17.

tax advantage Chapter 7 of this book discusses the forms of tax advantage: deferred taxes, tax-free income, and tax writeoffs.

tax-sheltered annuity (TSA) A tax-shelter plan available to teachers and to employees of non-profit organizations. See Chapter 8.

tax writeoff An expense, a loss, or another tax which, when incurred by a taxpayer, reduces taxable income. See Chapter 7.

term-insurance policy A life-insurance contract under which the insured pays only for pure insurance during a term stated in the contract. See Chapter 10.

theft insurance A *casualty insurance*; see *casualty insurance*.

track record The experience of a person or a business enterprise with respect to earnings and related qualities.

vehicle A property or operation suitable as an investment.

whole-life insurance A life-insurance contract under which the insured pays level premiums that include savings in addition to pure insurance. These premiums continue during the whole life of the insured. See Chapter 10. Also called *ordinary life insurance*.

SOME BUSINESS CONNECTIONS THAT HAVE HELPED

As I release this book for publication I wish to list for my readers a number of companies that have served me and my clients effectively during the past several years—companies that offer investment opportunities to the public in general, whose services and financial vehicles have been reliable during my past dealings with them.

REAL ESTATE PROGRAMS

BALCOR
10024 Skokie Blvd.
Skokie, IL 60077
(800) 323-2802

CAL WEST
2990 East La Palma Ave.
Anaheim, CA 92086
(714) 630-7407

CONSOLIDATED CAPITAL COMPANY
1900 Powell Street
Emeryville, CA 94608
(800) 772-2443

FOX & CARSKADON
2755 Campus Dr.
San Mateo, CA 94403
(415) 574-3333

PROPERTY RESOURCES
675 N. First St.
San Jose, CA 95112
(408) 294-5888

UNIVERSITY INVESTMENT MANAGEMENT COMPANY
666 E. Ocean Blvd.
Long Beach, CA 90802
(213) 435-6344

CABLE TELEVISION INVESTMENT PROGRAMS

JONES INTERCABLE
880 Continental National Bank Building
Englewood, CO 80110
(303) 761-3184

LIFE INSURANCE

ANCHOR NATIONAL LIFE INSURANCE COMPANY
2202 E. Camelback
Phoenix, AZ
(602) 955-0300

CAPITAL LIFE INSURANCE COMPANY
P.O. Box 1200
Denver, CO 80201
(303) 861-4065

COVENANT LIFE INSURANCE COMPANY
99 Woodland St.
Hartford CT 06101
(203) 249-9341

EXECUTIVE LIFE INSURANCE COMPANY
9777 Wilshire Blvd.
Beverly Hills, CA 90212
(213) 273-4202

FIREMAN'S FUND AMERICAN LIFE INSURANCE COMPANY
1600 Los Gamos Rd.
San Rafael, CA 94911
(415) 492-5252

KEMPER INVESTORS LIFE INSURANCE
120 S. LaSalle St.
Chicago, IL 60603
(312) 346-3223

UNIMARK, INC.
60 E. Sir Francis Drake Blvd.
Larkspur, CA 94939
(415) 461-4364

UNIVERSITY LIFE INSURANCE COMPANY
3500 W. DePauw Blvd.
Indianapolis, IN 46268
(317) 871-4302

GAS AND OIL PROGRAMS

DAMSON
Damson Securities Corp.
366 Madison Ave.
New York, NY 10017
(212) 697-1440

ECC RESOURCES
618 T. W. Patterson Blvd.
Fresno, CA 93721
(209) 485-8060

MISSION OIL COMPANY
P.O. Box 2300
Oakland, CA 94614
(415) 638-1800

PATRICK PETROLEUM COMPANY
Box 10
Bloomfield Hill, MI 48013
(800) 521-4353

PETRO LEWIS CORPORATION
717A Seventeenth Street
Denver, CO 80201
(303) 620-1000

DIAMONDS

INTERNATIONAL DIAMOND COMPANY
33 San Pablo Rd.
San Rafael, CA 94903
(415) 479-6060

ANNUITIES

ANCHOR NATIONAL LIFE INSURANCE COMPANY
2202 E. Camelback
Phoenix, AZ
(602) 955-0300

EXECUTIVE LIFE INSURANCE COMPANY
9777 Wilshire Blvd.
Beverly Hills, CA 90212
(213) 273-4202

FIREMAN'S FUND AMERICAN LIFE INSURANCE COMPANY
1600 Los Gamos Rd.
San Rafael, CA 94911
(415) 492-5252

KEMPER INVESTORS LIFE INSURANCE
120 S. LaSalle St.
Chicago, IL 60603
(312) 346-3223

UNIVERSITY LIFE INSURANCE COMPANY
3500 W. DePauw Blvd.
Indianapolis, IN 46268
(317) 871-4302

SAVER'S ANNUITIES

INTERMEDIATION, INC.
60 E. Sir Francis Drake Blvd.
Larkspur, CA 94939
(415) 461-4364

LEASING PROGRAMS

PHOENIX LEASING COMPANY
495 Miller Ave.
Mill Valley, CA 94941
(415) 383-9700

MINI-STORAGE AREA PROGRAM

PUBLIC STORAGE
94 S. Robles Ave.
Pasadena, CA 91101
(213) 681-6731

MOTEL PARTNERSHIPS

SUPER 8
P.O. Box 1456
Aberdeen, SD 57401
(800) 843-1960

COINS, GOLD, ETC.

COLBY GALLERIES
700 Larkspur Landing Circle, #199
Larkspur, CA 94939
(415) 457-8979

Standards of Professional Conduct of the International Association of Financial Planners, Inc.

A. *Compliance with Governing Laws and Regulations*

1. The financial planner shall have and maintain knowledge of and shall comply with applicable federal, state and provincial laws as well as applicable rules and regulations of any governmental agency governing his activity. The financial planner shall also comply with applicable rules and regulations of any organization exercising authority over his business activities.
2. The financial planner shall not knowingly participate in, assist, or condone any acts in violation of any statute or regulation, nor any act which would violate any provision of the Code of Ethics or these Standards of Professional Conduct.
3. A financial planner having supervisory responsibility shall exercise reasonable supervision over subordinate employees subject to his control, with a view to preventing any violations by such persons of applicable statutes, regulations, or provisions of the Code of Ethics or Standards of Professional Conduct.

B. *Recommendations to Clients*

1. The financial planner shall exercise diligence by thoroughly investigating the complete, unique circumstances of each client. In making recommendations, the financial planner shall be aware of and consider the appropriateness and suitability of such recom-

mendation based upon both present and future impact on the client.

2. The financial planner shall have a reasonable and adequate basis for any and all recommendations to clients. The financial planner shall maintain appropriate records to support the reasonableness of such recommendations and shall distinguish between facts and opinions in the presentation of recommendations. Such recommendations or actions shall be supported by appropriate research and investigation.

3. The financial planner shall scrupulously avoid any misleading statements, oral or written, regarding the expected results of any recommendation.

4. The financial planner shall act in a manner consistent with his obligation to deal fairly with all clients.

C. *Disclosure and Conflicts of Interest*

1. The financial planner shall inform his clients of compensation arrangements in connection with his services to them.

2. The financial planner shall be aware of the need to assist the client in obtaining professional counsel and advice where required. The financial planner shall avoid providing advice on any subject in which he is not professionally trained.

3. The financial planner when making recommendations, or when implementing a financial plan, shall disclose to clients any material conflict of interest which could reasonably be expected to impair the ability to render unbiased and objective advice. The financial planner shall also comply with all requirements as to disclosure of conflicts of interest imposed by law and by rules and regulations of organizations governing his activities.

D. *Priority of Transactions*

The financial planner shall conduct himself in such a manner that his clients have priority over personal interests, that personal interests do not operate adversely to the client's interests, and that he acts with impartiality with respect to all clients.

E. *Relationships with Others*

1. The financial planner shall take steps to promote among his associates and within his organization the existence and content of the Code of Ethics and of these Standards of Professional Conduct.

2. The financial planner shall act in a highly ethical and professional manner in his dealings with the public, his clients, his employees, his associates and fellow planners. The financial planner shall conduct himself in a fair and businesslike manner in all competitive business situations and shall adhere to the high standards of business conduct expected of financial planners. The financial planner shall not use his business position to influence fellow planners improperly on matters relating to their professional planners' organizations and shall respect the right of individual planners to hold varying viewpoints.

Note: The use of any gender herein shall include all genders and these standards of Professional Conduct shall be interpreted accordingly.

The Code of Ethics of the International Association of Financial Planners, Inc.

The reliance of the public and the business community on sound financial planning and advice imposes on the financial planning profession an obligation to maintain high standards of technical competence, morality and integrity. To this end, members of the International Association of Financial Planners, Inc. shall at all times maintain independence of thought and action; hold the affairs of their clients in strict confidence; strive continuously to improve their professional skills; promote sound financial planning; uphold the dignity and honor of the financial planning profession and maintain the highest standards of personal conduct.

In further recognition of the public interest and their obligation to the profession, members agree to adhere to the following principles of ethical conduct, the enumeration of which should not be construed as a denial of the existence of other standards of conduct not specifically mentioned:

Be devoted to continually improving their education in all aspects of financial planning and remain abreast of changing conditions affecting their clients' welfare;

Consult with others in situations requiring additional professional services and knowledge for their clients' best interest;

Oppose those who are deficient in moral character or professional competence, whose actions may cause financial harm to their clients;

Avoid association with anyone who does not comply with the spirit of these principles; and

Use the fact of membership in the International Association of Financial Planners, Inc. in an appropriate, non-commercial manner.

INDEX